Spanish Voices 2

Authentic Listening and Reading Practice in Spanish from Around Latin America and Spain

lingualism

© 2021 by Matthew Aldrich

The author's moral rights have been asserted.
All rights reserved. No part of this document may be reproduced or transmitted in any form or by any means, electronic, mechanical, photocopying, recording, or otherwise, without prior written permission of the publisher.

ISBN: 978-1-949650-67-9

Cover art: © daw666 / fotolia *and* © Jiri Kaderabek / dreamstime

website: www.lingualism.com

email: contact@lingualism.com

Table of Contents

Introduction iv
    What is *Spanish Voices*? iv
    How is *Spanish Voices* different? iv
    Can I benefit from this book at my level of Spanish? iv

How to Use This Book v
    Guidelines v
    The Texts and Translations vii
        Lines vii
        Fillers vii
        The Translations vii

Presentaciones 8
    1. Laura 8
    2. Jorge 5
    3. Sandra 9
    4. José 12

    5. Francisco 16

    6. Florencia 20

Rutinas Diarias **24**

    7. La Rutina Diaria de Laura 24

    8. La Rutina Diaria de Jorge 28

    9. La Rutina Diaria de Sandra 32

    10. La Rutina Diaria de José 36

Recuerdos de la Infancia **40**

    11. El Cometa 40

    12. Un Día Cualquiera de Cuando Era Niño 44

Vacaciones **48**

    13. Unas Vacaciones en Francia 48

    14. Trujillo 52

    15. Buzios 56

Mi Ciudad **60**

    16. La Ciudad de México 60

    17. Madrid 64

    18. Buenos Aires 68

La Cultura **73**

    19. El Fútbol en Costa Rica 73

    20. El Turismo en Perú 78

    21. Espanglish 82

    22. La Religión en Honduras 86

    23. El Cine Español 90

    24. Los Casamientos Argentinos 94

Temas Sociales **99**

    25. El Sistema de Salud en Costa Rica 99

    26. La Pobreza 103

    27. La Discriminación 107

    28. La Migración Ilegal de Niños 111

    29. La Violencia Doméstica 115

30. La Economía de Argentina *119*

notes **124**

Accompanying audio and online resources are available at:

www.lingualism.com/sv2

All segments from *Spanish Voices 1* and *Spanish Voices 2*

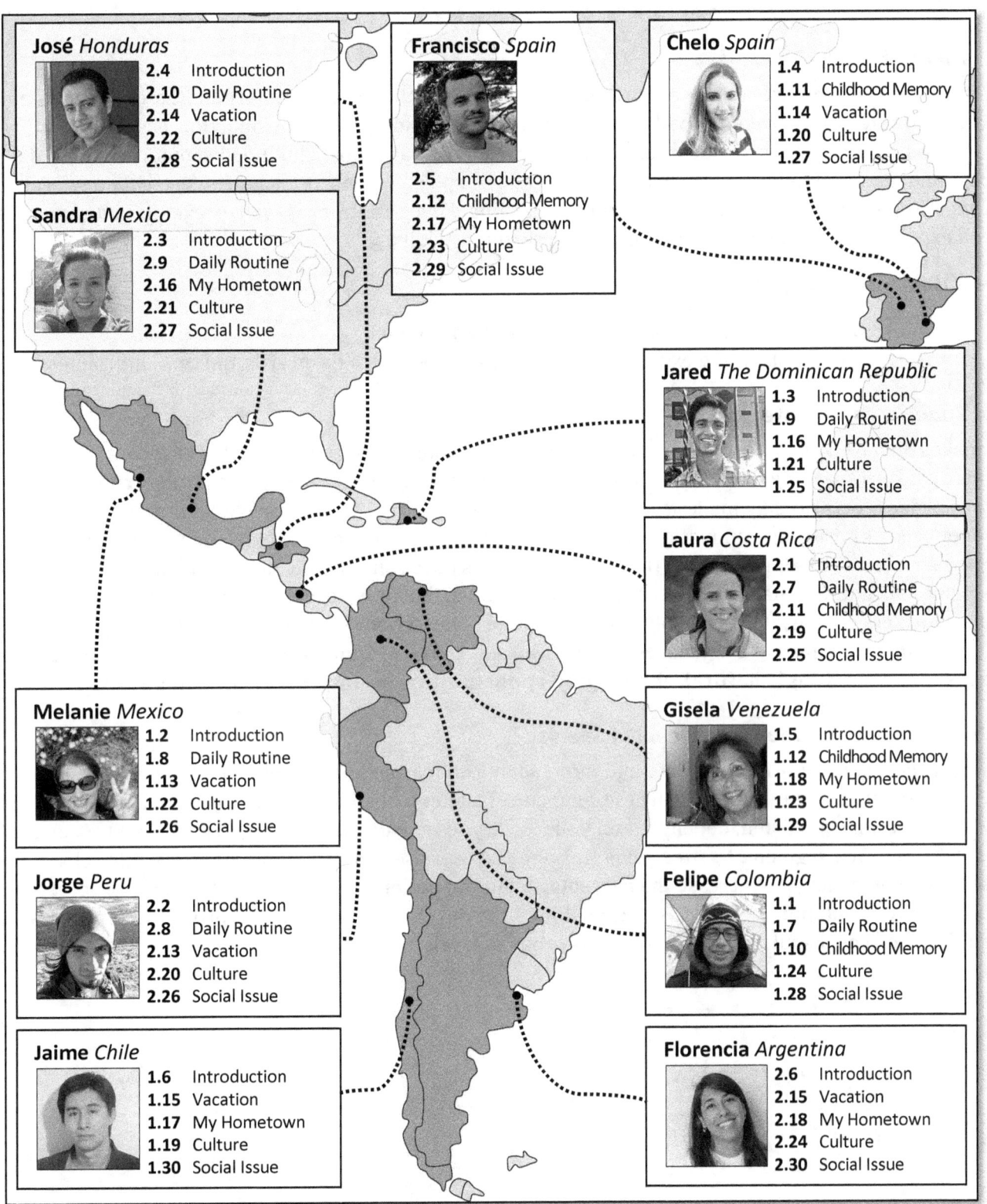

Introduction

What is *Spanish Voices*?

Spanish Voices is a two-part series of short audio essays by contributors from around Latin America and Spain. Each speaker has provided a total of five audio essays, including a self-introduction, essays on cultural and social issues, as well as various personal topics such as vacations, childhood memories, their daily routines, and their hometowns. Each book features six speakers and 30 audio essay chapters, called *segments*. A segment consists of a transcription (text), English translation, as well as exercises designed to help you expand your vocabulary and improve your listening skills.

On **www.lingualism.com/sv2** you can:

- download or stream the accompanying audio tracks for **free**.
- practice the vocabulary and expressions with online interactive flashcards, quizzes, and games.

How is *Spanish Voices* different?

What makes *Spanish Voices* a unique and powerful learning tool is that the material is based on recordings of native speakers speaking naturally and off-the-cuff—*not* voice actors reading prepared scripts. You will hear the speakers occasionally make what you are sure are mistakes; and you're likely right. Words may be mispronounced or misused; grammatical rules may not always be followed; sentences may be left unfinished if the speaker decides to rephrase what they are saying. This poses an extra challenge for listening. However, it is also very insightful to hear natural, spoken Spanish at various speeds, in all its varieties, and by a range of native speakers. This is, unfortunately, something most coursebooks lack in favor of carefully prepared, unnaturally slow listenings in a neutral accent. **It is hoped that the *Spanish Voices* series fills this gap to provide some refreshingly natural, challenging opportunities for improving listening skills.**

Can I benefit from this book at my level of Spanish?

This book is best suited for intermediate and more advanced learners. However, even lower-level students can benefit from listening to and studying the segments. Just keep in mind that the goal is ***not*** to understand 100%. The first time you listen, depending on your level, you may understand, say, 1%, 10%, 50%, or 90% of what you hear in a segment. If, after going through the exercises and studying the text while relistening several times, you manage to increase the percentage you can understand, you will have made progress and are successfully developing your skills and pushing your level up. Taking this approach, the material in *Spanish Voices* can be useful to learners at a wide range of levels.

How to Use This Book

To get the most out of this book, you need to exercise a bit of **discipline**—discipline to resist reading the texts and their translations before you have thoroughly studied the listenings. This cannot be emphasized enough. Once you have read the texts and translations, the dynamics of what you can obtain from listening to the segments change fundamentally. You should first listen to a segment *several* times while working your way through the exercises. These have been designed to help you first understand the gist and gradually discover details as you relisten. Only once you have come to understand as much as you can through the exercises should you move on to study the text and translation that follow. This approach will result in maximum efficiency in improving your listening skills. A step-by-step guideline follows:

Guidelines

1. **CHOOSE A SEGMENT TO STUDY:** The segments can be studied in any order; however, there is somewhat of a gradual progression from shorter and slower segments to longer and faster segments through each book. The box to the right of the segment's title shows the speaker's name and country of origin, as well as the number of words in the audio essay and the rate of speech the speaker uses (words per minute). The MP3s that accompany *Spanish Voices* are available as free downloads at **www.lingualism.com/sv2**.
2. **TITLE AND KEY WORDS:** *Before you listen the first time, be sure to read the title of the segment and look over the "True or False" questions.* Going into a listening "blind"—without having any context, without even knowing the topic—makes listening comprehension in a foreign language extremely difficult. Just by knowing the general topic, we are able to improve the amount we can understand, as we are able to draw on knowledge from our past experiences, anticipate what might be said, recognize known words, and guess new words and phrases.
3. **TRUE OR FALSE:** *Answer the "True or False" questions.* (Do not read ahead to the multiple-choice questions as some of these questions themselves may answer the true-false questions.) If you feel unsure of your answers, listen to the audio again before checking your answers. You will notice that a small number follows most answers in the answer key. These numbers correspond to the line number in the text and translation that reveals the answer. If you do not understand *why* you got an answer wrong, quickly look at the text and/or translation for that line number. (Here's where you have to use your self-discipline *not* to read beyond the specified line number!) Listen again and place a check next to each *true or false* question as you hear the answer.
4. **EXPRESSIONS:** *Match the Spanish words and phrases to their English translations.* The vocabulary focuses mostly on high-frequency adverbs, connectors, and phrases. You will learn by spending time playing with the words, trying to match them up by process of elimination and educated guesses. So don't look up the answers too quickly! After you've matched the words and checked your answers, listen again while you check off the items as you hear them.
5. **MULTIPLE CHOICE:** *Answer the "Multiple Choice" questions.* Follow the same guidelines as for the *true or false* questions. Note that both the *true or false* and *multiple-choice* questions are based on

information found in the segment, according to the information provided by the speaker, regardless of the accuracy of the information. You can think of each question as being preceded by "According to *the speaker*,..." or "*The speaker* mentions that...".

6. **TEXT AND TRANSLATION:** Now that you've worked your way through the first three exercises and have managed to pick up more of what has been said, you can feel free to move on to study the text and translation for the segment. This part is more *free-style*. Depending on your level of Spanish and level of comfort with the text, you can approach this in several ways. For instance, you can cover the Spanish side and first read the translation; then try to translate the English back into Spanish based on what you remember. Also, you can simply try to brainstorm some possible Spanish equivalents for the words or phrases in the English translation; then check the Spanish side and see how it was actually said. Conversely, you can cover the English side first and relisten while you read along with the Spanish, perhaps pausing the audio to repeat each line aloud. In any case, the side-by-side arrangement of the Spanish text and its English translation allows you to cover one side and test yourself in various ways. You should be able to match up most words and phrases with their equivalents in English. You may want to highlight useful and interesting vocabulary and phrases you want to learn.

7. **VOCABULARY:** Following the text and translation are two more exercises, which can be done while looking back at the text when needed. The "Vocabulary" exercise presents English translations for at least ten Spanish key words and phrases found in the segment. You can replay the audio while listening for the Spanish equivalents, and if needed, look back at the text. Each vocabulary item is followed by a reference to the line number where the Spanish word or phrase appears.

8. **TRANSLATE:** The "Translate" exercise requires two steps. First, you must circle the correct word(s) to complete each sentence. The purpose is to draw your attention to collocations and idioms and develop the very important skill of noticing *how* words are used together in sentences. The answer key shows the line number of the text where the structure in question can be found. The focus is on the little words—prepositions and pronouns, as well as verb forms such as the subjunctive. The second step is to translate the sentences into English. You will find suggested English translations in the answer key. Keep in mind that there is always more than one way to translate a sentence.

9. **LISTEN AGAIN:** Try listening to the segments you have already studied again later. You will find that you can understand more and with more ease the following day. (Studies have shown that material learned is consolidated and organized in the brain during sleep.)

The Texts and Translations

Lines
The text and translation for each segment have been divided into numbered "lines," which are not necessarily complete sentences or even clauses but are manageable chunks that can be studied.

Fillers
Fillers, which are used to signal that the speaker is thinking of what to say next, are a common and natural part of spoken language. Fillers vary from speaker and region. The most common and universal, are eh… and em…. Other popular fillers include bueno, este…, pues, entonces. Keep your ears open for such words and how native speakers use them. Another trait of spoken discourse is that the speaker may misspeak, then back up to correct themselves. Also, a speaker may decide to rephrase a sentence or simply not finish it. These are all marked with ellipses (…) so that you can easily see that the *word* you didn't catch is, in fact, not a complete word at all. These ellipses are meant to aid you in deciphering the listening. However, when you are reading for meaning, anything before an ellipsis can be ignored.

The Translations
Good style has been sacrificed in favor of direct translations so that Spanish words and phrases can easily be matched up to their translations. You are encouraged to think of alternative ways lines could be translated into English.

Presentaciones

Laura

Laura (Costa Rica)
430 words (141 wpm) 1

True or False

1. Laura is 26 years old. T☐ F☐
2. Her husband is a web developer. T☐ F☐
3. She works with an American Company. T☐ F☐
4. She studied drama in college. T☐ F☐
5. She only takes care of dogs (and not other animals). T☐ F☐

Expressions

a veces	a lot of
básicamente	actually
bueno	also
como	always
demasiado	basically
en realidad	because
entonces	but
hasta	even
la mayoría de las veces	I'm from
luego	like
muchas gracias	lots of
muchos	most of the time
obviamente	obviously
pero	once
porque	so (much), too (much)
siempre	so, therefore
soy de	sometimes
también	thanks a lot
tienen que ir	then
un montón de	they have to go
una vez	well

Multiple Choice

1. Laura has ___.

    a. one son c. two daughters
    b. two sons d. two sons and one daughter

2. Laura and her husband have been married for ___ years.

    a. two   b. eight   c. twelve   d. fifteen

3. Which of the following is true about Laura?

    a. She has a pet turtle.   c. She likes reading.
    b. She is a web designer.   d. Her husband is Canadian.

Text

¡Hola! ¿Cómo están?	1	Hi! How are you?
Mi nombre es Laura.	2	My name is Laura.
Tengo treinta y seis años.	3	I am 36 years old.
Y yo soy de Costa Rica.	4	And I am from Costa Rica.
Vivo en San José, Costa Rica con mis hijos y mi esposo.	5	I live in San José, Costa Rica, with my kids and my husband.
Tengo dos chicos: Tomás, que tiene once, y Oscar, que tiene nueve.	6	I have two boys: Tomas, who is eleven years old, and Oscar, nine years old.
Y bueno, obviamente son la vida entera mía.	7	And well, obviously, they are my whole life.
Son mi amor; los amo con todo mi corazón.	8	They are my love; I love them with all my heart.
Son unos niños súper lindos, súper buenos.	9	They are really cute boys, really good boys.
Van a la escuela y siempre están con buenas notas.	10	They go to school and get really good grades.
Y no lo digo porque yo soy la mamá. ¡Son buenos chicos!	11	And I am not saying all this because I am their mom. They [really] are good kids!
Y mi esposo, que se llama Chalo	12	And my husband, whose name is Chalo
—bueno, en realidad se llama Gonzalo, pero le dicen Chalo—	13	—well, actually, his name is Gonzalo, but everybody calls him Chalo—
él es diseñador web y también se dedica a la fotografía.	14	he is a web developer and also a photographer.
Y con él tenemos doce años de estar casados.	15	And we have been married for 12 years.
Bueno, y a mí, ¿de mí qué puedo contar?	16	And what can I tell you about myself?
Que me encantan un montón de cosas,	17	I love to do a lot of things,
pero bueno, mi trabajo es: hago traducciones.	18	but my job: I am a translator.
Trabajo con una compañía canadiense.	19	I work with a Canadian company.
Entonces, traduzco todo el contenido que siempre andan produciendo del francés al español, y a veces de inglés al español.	20	So, my job is to translate all their content from French to Spanish, and sometimes from English to Spanish.
Entonces, a eso casi siempre me dedico las primeras horas de la mañana.	21	So, that is what I'm usually doing early in the morning.
Luego también soy actriz de teatro,	22	And I am also a theater actress,
entonces ahí andamos siempre como locos ensayando, que la producción, que la presentación, que…	23	so we are always running around like crazy rehearsing, producing, presenting,…
Bueno, es demasiado divertido y me fascina.	24	Anyway, it is so much fun, and I love it.
Eso fue lo que estudié en la universidad: drama.	25	That is actually what I studied in college: drama.

Entonces, bueno, eso es mi, mi, lo que amo en el corazón hacer.	26	So, well, that is me, what I really love to do in my heart.
Luego también me encanta, bueno, me encantan hacer un montón de cosas.	27	Then, also, there are a lot of things I love, well, love to do.
Me gusta cocinar, inventar cosas nuevas y revolver cosas.	28	I love to cook—invent new things and mix up things.
Y mis hijos y mi esposo son los que tienen que andar probando lo que yo hago,	29	My husband and kids are the ones that have to try my recipes,
pero la mayoría de las veces sale bien, ¡espero!	30	but most of the time, they turn out okay, I hope!
Bueno, ¡eso es lo que dicen!	31	Or at least that what they say!
Me gusta leer—ando viendo que leo.	32	I love to read. I am always searching for something to read.
Me encanta ver series de televisión, muchas.	33	I also enjoy watching TV series, lots of them.
Me encanta el ciclismo.	34	I love cycling.
Y cada vez que puedo, así como los fines de semana sobre todo, lo primero que hago es abrir los ojos y agarrar la bicicleta y me voy.	35	Every time I can, like on weekends especially, the first thing I do is open my eyes, grab my bike and go somewhere.
Y ese es así, como el tiempo para mí, mi tiempo de relajarme, ¡entonces me gusta!	36	That is like "my time," time for me, my time to relax; I love it!
También me encantan los animales.	37	I also love animals.
Tengo una pequeña guardería de perritos.	38	I have a small pet sitting company.
Cuido perritos cuando los dueños se van de vacaciones,	39	I take care of doggies when their owners are away on vacation,
o se tienen que ir por algún motivo o no los pueden cuidar durante el día,	40	or they go away for some reason, or they can't take care of them during the day,
entonces me los dejan a mí y yo cuido perritos!	41	so they leave them with me. So I am a doggie sitter!
O los camino también, los saco a caminar...	42	I also walk them, take them out for walks.
Y gatos y bueno de todo me han dejado, ¡hasta una vez una tortuga!	43	And I've also taken care of cats, and well anything, even a turtle once!
Y bueno, ¡básicamente eso es!	44	That's it, basically!
¡Esa soy yo y muchas gracias por escucharme!	45	That's me! And thanks a lot for listening to me!

Vocabulary

1. kids[5] _____
2. whole[7] _____
3. love[8] _____
4. cute[9] _____
5. grade[10] _____
6. to be married[15] _____
7. to tell[16] _____
8. job[18] _____
9. morning[21] _____
10. crazy[23] _____
11. husband[29] _____
12. to grab[35] _____
13. time[36] _____
14. owner[39] _____
15. to take care of[40] _____
16. turtle[43] _____
17. to listen[45] _____

Translate

1. Ellos van *a / en* la escuela.
2. Chalo se *dedica / dedicata* a la fotografía.
3. Tienen doce años *de estar / estado* casados.
4. Laura es *actriz / actora* de teatro.
5. Yo *estudié / estudió* drama en la escuela.
6. Me gusta *leer / leyendo*.

notes

True or False: 1. F[3] 2. T[14] 3. F[19] 4. T[25] 5. F[43] **Expressions:** a veces - sometimes / básicamente - basically / bueno - well / como - like / demasiado - so (much), too (much) / en realidad - actually / entonces - so, therefore / hasta - even / la mayoría de las veces - most of the time / luego - then / muchas gracias - thanks a lot / muchos - lots of / obviamente - obviously / pero - but / porque - because / siempre - always / soy de - I'm from / también - also / tienen que ir - they have to go / un montón de - a lot of / una vez - once **Multiple Choice:** 1. b[6] 2. c[15] 3. c[32] **Vocabulary:** 1. hijos 2. entero 3. amor 4. lindo 5. nota 6. estar casado 7. contar 8. trabajo 9. mañana 10. loco 11. esposo 12. agarrar 13. tiempo 14. dueño 15. cuidar 16. tortuga 17. escuchar **Translate:** 1. a[10] They go to school. 2. dedica[14] Chalo is dedicated to photography. 3. de estar[15] They have been married for twelve years. 4. actriz[22] Laura is a theater actress. 5. estudié[25] I studied drama at school. 6. leer[32] I like reading.

Jorge

Jorge (Peru)
385 words (120 wpm) 2

True or False

1. Jorge gave private English lessons. T☐ F☐
2. He studied gastronomy in high school. T☐ F☐
3. When he was younger, he spent most of his free time hanging out with his friends. T☐ F☐
4. He likes going to the gym. T☐ F☐
5. He thinks that sports are his true calling. T☐ F☐

Expressions

a comparación de	alongside
a la vez	at the same time
actualmente	compared to
conveniente	currently
en paralelo	handy
encontré mi verdadera vocación	I found my true calling
físicamente	I'm a cinema buff
nada	nothing, not at all
soy amante del cine	physically
tal	such

Multiple Choice

1. Which of the following is true?
    a. Jorge lives with two friends.
    b. Jorge is an English teacher now.
    c. Jorge's house is in the north of the city.
    d. Jorge's major was English.

2. Jorge says that his work experience in the hostel was ___.
    a. awful because he couldn't understand what people were saying
    b. amazing because he loves meeting new people and cultures
    c. horrible because the guest always left their rooms dirty
    d. *none of the above*

3. Which of the following is not true about Jorge?
    a. He doesn't like cooking for friends.
    b. He has worked as a translator.
    c. He recently left a job.
    d. He speaks English well.

Text

Hola! Soy Jorge. Tengo 26 años.	1	Hi! I'm Jorge. I'm 26 years old.
Soy Peruano y nací en Lima.	2	I am Peruvian, and I was born in Lima.
Actualmente vivo en la casa de mis padres.	3	I'm currently living in my parents' house.
La comparto con ellos y con mis otros dos hermanos.	4	I share it with them and with my two other brothers.
Eh... mi casa está ubicada al sur de la ciudad muy cerca del mar, cosa que es genial en verano,	5	Uh... My home is located to the south of the city quite near the sea, which is great in the summer,
porque el clima es súper fresco y soleado,	6	because the weather is super cool and sunny,
aunque en invierno puede ser completamente lo opuesto,	7	although in the winter it can be completely the opposite
ya que en Lima la humedad es muy alta y el frío que se siente es nada agradable.	8	since in Lima the humidity is very high, and the cold you feel is not at all nice.
Cuando yo estaba en la escuela mi madre me hizo tomar clases de inglés en paralelo a mi secundaria, por casi cuatro años.	9	When I was in school, my mother made me take English classes alongside high school for almost four years.
Cuando yo me gradué de la secundaria a la vez justo también terminé mis estudios de inglés.	10	When I graduated from high school, at the very same time, I also finished my studies in English.
Esa es mi primera carrera.	11	That was my first major.
Después de eso yo comencé a dar clases de inglés privadas.	12	After that, I started giving private English classes.
Y a la vez si tenía la oportunidad, hacía trabajos de traducción.	13	And at the same time, if I had the opportunity, I would do translation jobs.
Años después de eso encontré mi verdadera vocación, que es la cocina.	14	Years after that, I found my true calling, namely cooking.
Estudié cuatro años en una escuela de gastronomía en Lima.	15	I studied at a gastronomy school in Lima for four years.
Eh... después de eso trabajé en varios lugares.	16	Uh... after that worked in several places.
Eh... trabajé en varios restaurantes, en un hotel muy grande en Lima.	17	Uh... I worked in several restaurants in a big hotel in Lima.
Hice eventos, buffets para eventos.	18	I did events, buffets for events.
Y después de eso tuve un trabajo por cuatro casi cinco años, que es el último que dejé hace poco.	19	And after that, I had a job for four, almost five, years, which is the last one; I just recently left it.
Trabajé en un hospedaje de turistas.	20	I worked at a hostel.
Fue una experiencia muy increíble y única,	21	It was a very amazing and unique experience
porque es como viajar sin moverse prácticamente ¿no?	22	because it's practically like traveling without moving, right?
Tienes la oportunidad de conocer mucha gente alrededor del mundo.	23	You have the opportunity to meet many people from around the world.
Y el hecho de yo supiera inglés fue muy, muy conveniente,	24	And the fact that I knew English was really, really handy

porque me pude... me podía comunicar de tal manera y con tal facilidad con todo el mundo.	25	because I was able... I could communicate in such a way and with such ease with everyone.	
En mi tiempo libre a mí me gusta salir con mis amigos.	26	In my spare time, I like going out with my friends.	
Soy una persona muy amante del cine.	27	I'm a real cinema buff.	
Eh... a comparación de infancia que fue muy tranquila y pasiva, y muy de estar metido en casa,	28	Uh... compared to my childhood that was very quiet and passive, and mostly about being at home,	
ahora me gusta hacer completamente lo opuesto.	29	now I like to do the complete opposite,	
Soy una persona más físicamente activa.	30	I am a more physically active person.	
Me gustan los deportes; me gusta ir al gimnasio regularmente, mantenerme en forma.	31	I like sports. I like going to the gym regularly, staying in shape.	
Eh... y también lo que me gusta bastante como hobby es esto... eh... ir a la casa de amigos,	32	Uh... and also what I like to do a lot as a hobby is either uh... go to friends' houses,	
y poder eh... cocinarles a ellos.	33	and get to cook for them.	
Es algo que disfruto más que cocinar para mismo.	34	That's something I enjoy more than cooking for myself.	
Es un poco... es un poco irónico a veces ¿no?	35	It's a little... it's a bit ironic sometimes, isn't it?	

Vocabulary

1. great[5] _____
2. sunny _____
3. cool[6] _____
4. humidity[8] _____
5. to take classes[9] _____
6. high school[10] _____
7. hostel[20] _____
8. amazing[21] _____
9. spare time[26] _____
10. opposite[29] _____
11. gym[31] _____
12. staying in shape[31] _____

Translate

1. El clima es súper fresco y *soleado / solado*.
2. La humedad / *humedidad* es muy alta y el frío que se siente es nada agradable.
3. Cuando yo *me / -* gradué de la secundaria a la vez justo también terminé mis estudios de inglés.
4. Después de eso yo comencé *a dar / dando* clases de inglés privadas.
5. Yo *hice / hací* buffets para eventos.
6. Es algo que disfruto más *que / de* cocinar para mi mismo.

notes

True or False: 1. T[12] 2. F[15] 3. F[28] 4. T[30] 5. F[31] **Expressions:** a comparación de - compared to / a la vez - at the same time / actualmente - currently / conveniente - handy / en paralelo - alongside / encontré mi verdadera vocación - I found my true calling / fisicamente - physically / nada - nothing, not at all / soy amante del cine - I'm a cinema buff / tal - such **Multiple Choice:** 1. d[11] 2. b[21] 3. a[33] **Vocabulary:** 1. genial 2. soleado 3. fresco 4. humedad 5. tomar clases 6. (escuela) secundaria 7. hospedaje de turistas 8. increíble 9. tiempo libre 10. opuesto 11. gimnasio 12. mantenerse en forma **Translate:** 1. soleado[6] The climate is super cool and sunny. 2. humedad[8] The humidity is very high, and the cold you feel is nothing at all nice. 3. me[10] When I graduated from high school, at the very same time, I also finished my studies in English. 4. a dar[12] After that, I started to give private English classes. 5. hice[18] I did buffets for events. 6. que[34] It is something that I enjoy more than cooking for myself.

Sandra

Sandra (Mexico)
260 words (125 wpm)   3

True or False

1. Sandra has been living in the U.S. for four years.   T ☐ F ☐
2. She has a three-year-old son.   T ☐ F ☐
3. She decided to go back to school in order to improve her Spanish.   T ☐ F ☐
4. She is currently taking English classes.   T ☐ F ☐
5. Sandra and her family like to play boardgames.   T ☐ F ☐

Expressions

al mismo tiempo	all types of
de esta forma	at the same time
durante	board game
juego de mesa	for (duration)
nos levantamos temprano	in this way
todo tipo de	to work from home
trabajar desde casa	we get up early

Multiple Choice

1. Sandra likes her job because ___.
   a. she has a lot of free time
   b. she can help people
   c. she earns a lot of money
   d. she can work from home

2. Which of the following is true about Sandra?
   a. Her mother lives with them.
   b. She loves doing puzzles.
   c. She is an accountant.
   d. She loves going to the mountains with her family.

3. Sandra's favorite genre of movie is ___.
   a. horror
   b. romantic comedy
   c. fantasy
   d. action

Text

¡Hola! Mi nombre es Sandra y tengo 33 años.	1	Hello! My name is Sandra, and I am 33 years old.
Yo soy de la Ciudad de México pero actualmente vivo en los Estados Unidos.	2	I am from Mexico City, but I now live in the United States.
He vivido en los Estados Unidos durante cuatro años,	3	I have lived in the United States for four years,
y actualmente vivo en la ciudad de Galveston en Texas.	4	and I currently live in the City of Galveston in Texas.
Yo vivo aquí con mi esposo y con mi hijo de 3 años.	5	I live here with my husband and with my son, who is three years old.
Yo estudié contaduría y trabajé en esta área por aproximadamente seis años,	6	I studied Accounting, and I worked in this area for about six years,

9 | Spanish Voices 2

pero después decidí regresar a la escuela para ser maestra de español.	7	but later I decided to go back to school to become a Spanish teacher.
Y esto es lo que actualmente hago; actualmente soy maestra de español,	8	And that's what I currently do; I am currently a Spanish teacher,
y es algo que me gusta mucho y disfruto mucho.	9	and it's something that I like very much, and I enjoy a lot.
Este trabajo también me da la oportunidad de trabajar desde casa,	10	This job gives me the opportunity as well to work from home,
y de esta forma puedo estar con mi hijo y al mismo tiempo trabajar.	11	and in this way, I can be with my son and work at the same time.
En mi tiempo libre me gusta ver películas.	12	In my free time, I like to watch movies.
Las películas que me gustan son la de terror y las de misterio.	13	The movies I like are horror movies and mystery ones.
También me gusta leer; me gusta leer todo tipo de novelas.	14	I also like reading. I like reading all types of novels.
Otra cosa que me gusta hacer es… me gusta hacer rompecabezas,	15	Another thing I like doing is, I like to do puzzles.
y también me gusta andar en bicicleta.	16	And I also like riding bicycles.
Em… los fines de semana me gusta pasar tiempo con mi familia.	17	Um… on the weekends, I like to spend time with my family.
Regularmente lo que hacemos los fines de semana mi familia y yo es ir a la playa.	18	What we usually do on the weekends, my family and I, is go to the beach.
Nos levantamos temprano y nos vamos a la playa, y pasamos ahí toda la mañana.	19	We wake up early, and we go to the beach, and we spend there all morning
Y ya por la tarde nos… nos regresamos… nos regresamos a casa y pasamos tiempo aquí en familia.	20	and in the afternoon we… we come back, we come back home, and we spend time here as a family.
Regularmente vemos una película o a veces jugamos algún juego de mesa.	21	We usually watch a movie or sometimes we play some board game.
Y eso es lo que hacemos los fines de semana.	22	And that's what we do on the weekends.

Vocabulary

1. currently[2] _____
2. accounting[6] _____
3. later[7] _____
4. what _____
5. to work from home[10] _____
6. novel[14] _____
7. puzzles[15] _____
8. weeknd[17] _____
9. to spend (time)[19] _____
10. board game[21] _____

Translate

1. He vivido en los Estados Unidos *durante / para* algunos años.
2. Y después decidí *- / de* regresar a la escuela.
3. Puedo estar con mi hijo y *al / en el* mismo tiempo trabajar.
4. En mi tiempo libre me *gusta / gustan* ver películas.
5. Me gusta leer *todo tipo / todos tipos* de novelas.
6. También me gusta andar *en / por* bicicleta.

notes

True or False: 1. T³ 2. T⁵ 3. F⁷ 4. F⁸ 5. T²¹ **Expressions:** al mismo tiempo - at the same time / de esta forma - in this way / durante - for (duration) / juego de mesa - board game / nos levantamos temprano - we get up early / todo tipo de - all types of / trabajar desde casa - to work from home **Multiple Choice:** 1. d¹⁰ 2. b¹⁵ 3. a¹³ **Vocabulary:** 1. actualmente 2. contaduría 3. después 4. lo que 5. trabajar desde casa 6. novela 7. rompecabezas 8. fin de semana 9. pasar 10. juego de mesa **Translate:** 1. durante³ I have lived in the United States for a few years. 2. -⁷ And then I decided to return to school. 3. al¹¹ I can be with my son and work at the same. 4. gusta¹² In my free time, I like to watch movies. 5. todo tipo¹⁴ I like to read all kinds of novels. 6. en¹⁶ I also like to ride a bicycle.

José

José (Honduras)
308 words (140 wpm) 4

True or False

1. José works as a physician in the department of scientific research. T☐ F☐
2. He wants to find a new job as soon as possible. T☐ F☐
3. He likes singing but he doesn't like listening to music. T☐ F☐
4. He likes spending most of his spare time at home. T☐ F☐
5. He doesn't have a favorite genre of books. T☐ F☐

Expressions

cualquier tipo	all the rest
de alguna forma	any kind
docencia	country
felizmente	happily
frecuentemente	I've been doing it for five years
la verdad que	it excites me a lot
llevo cinco años en hacer esto	it is located
lo que más me gusta hacer	often
me apasiona mucho	on-about
patria	somehow
se localiza	teaching
sobre	the truth is that
todo lo demás	useful
útil	what I like to do most

Multiple Choice

1. José has ___.

    a. three sons
    b. three daughters
    c. one son and two daughters
    d. two sons and one daughter

2. Which of the following is true about José?

    a. He hates long trips.
    b. He only reads non-fiction books.
    c. He's divorced.
    d. He composes music.

3. José says that he wants to improve his professional skills in order to ___.

    a. make his children proud of him
    b. do something useful for his country
    c. plan for his future and retirement
    d. find a better job

Text

¡Hola! Me llamo José.	1	Hi! My name is Jose.
Tengo treinta y cuatro años de edad.	2	I'm 34 years old.
Vivo en la ciudad de La Lima en Cortés, Honduras.	3	I live in the city of La Lima in Cortés, Honduras.
En realidad soy originario de la ciudad de La Ceiba, que es una ciudad muy hermosa que se localiza en el litoral atlántico de mi país.	4	Actually, I'm originally from the city of La Ceiba, which is a very beautiful city located on the Atlantic coast of my country.
Está bañada por el mar Caribe.	5	It's bordered by the Caribbean Sea.
Tengo… ya les dije que tengo treinta y cuatro años de edad.	6	I'm… I told you that I'm 34 years old.
Estoy felizmente casado.	7	I am happily married.
Tengo tres hijos:	8	I have three children:
un varón de ocho años, uno de cinco años y un pequeñín de dos años y medio.	9	an eight-year-old boy, a five-year-old [boy], and a two-and-a-half-year-old toddler.
La verdad que los disfruto mucho.	10	I really enjoy them a lot.
Disfruto mucho pasar tiempo con ellos.	11	I so enjoy spending time with them.
Eh… Me gusta verlos jugar, verlos crecer, aun verse pelear y todo lo demás.	12	Uh… I like watching them play, watching them grow, even watching them fight and all the rest.
Mi carrera es la docencia.	13	My career is teaching.
Soy profesor de secundaria.	14	I am a high school teacher.
Enseño las clases de ciencias naturales (física, química y biología) a estudiantes de secundaria.	15	I teach classes in natural science (physics, chemistry, and biology) to high school students.
Eh… llevo en la carrera quince años,	16	Uh… I've been in this line of work for fifteen years,
y espero poder seguir ejerciendo porque es algo que sí me apasiona mucho.	17	and I hope I can continue to practice it because it is something that excites me a lot.
Dentro de mis actividades, lo que más me gusta hacer es cantar… es la música.	18	Among my pastimes, what I like to do most is sing… is music.
Me gusta mucho escuchar música.	19	I love listening to music.
Componer música también me gusta mucho,	20	I also really like composing music,
aunque no lo hago tan frecuentemente.	21	although I don't do this very often.
Me gusta mucho salir; me gusta mucho viajar,	22	I really like going out; I like traveling a lot,
agarrar un vehículo y viajar, ir a alguna ciudad.	23	taking a vehicle and traveling, going to some city.
La verdad que cuando voy de viaje, la parte que más disfruto es el viaje, no el llegar al lugar.	24	The truth is that when I travel, the part I enjoy most is the journey, not getting there.
Así que es una actividad que me gusta mucho.	25	So it's something I really like to do.
En mi tiempo libre me gusta estar en el Internet.	26	In my free time, I like to be on the Internet.
Me gusta mucho navegar en Internet, leer libros.	27	I like surfing the Internet, reading books.

Leo libros de cualquier tipo.	28	I read books of any kind.
Pueden ser historias de ficción; pueden ser libros sobre motivación,	29	They may be fictional stories; they may be books on motivation,
libros sobre cualquier tema que sea interesante.	30	books on any subject that is interesting.
Espero en el futuro seguir ejerciendo la docencia,	31	I hope in the future to continue teaching,
profesionalizarme más en la carrera para poder de alguna forma impactar mi país,	32	developing myself in this field to somehow have an impact on my country,
de alguna forma educar mentes y poder ser útil a mi patria.	33	to somehow educate minds and to be useful to my country.

Vocabulary

1. bordered by[5] _____
2. toddler[9] _____
3. son[9] _____
4. to fight[12] _____
5. to play[12] _____
6. to grow[12] _____
7. career[13] _____
8. teacher, professor[14] _____
9. to teach[15] _____
10. to continue to[17] _____
11. to sing[18] _____
12. to take[23] _____
13. journey[24] _____
14. to surf the web[27] _____
15. fictional stories[29] _____
16. to keep (doing)[31] _____

Translate

1. La isla está bañada *por el / del* mar Caribe.
2. Ya les *dije / he dedido* que tengo treinta y cuatro años de edad.
3. Llevo *en / de* esa carrera quince años.
4. Espero poder seguir *ejerciendo / ejercer* porque es algo que sí me apasiona mucho.
5. Cuando voy de viaje, la parte que más disfruto es el viaje, no *el / lo* llegar al lugar.
6. Me gusta leer libros sobre cualquier tema que *sea / es* interesante.

notes

True or False: 1. F[12] 2. F[17] 3. F[19] 4. F[22] 5. T[28] **Expressions:** cualquier tipo - any kind / de alguna forma - somehow / docencia - teaching / felizmente - happily / frecuentemente - often / la verdad que - the truth is that / llevo cinco años en hacer esto - I've been doing it for five years / lo que más me gusta hacer - what I like to do most / me apasiona mucho - it excites me a lot / patria - country / se localiza - it is located / sobre - on-about / todo lo demás - all the rest / útil - useful **Multiple Choice:** 1. a[8] 2. d[20] 3. b[32] **Vocabulary:** 1. bañado por 2. pequeñín 3. hijo varón 4. pelear 5. jugar 6. crecer 7. carrera 8. profesor 9. enseñar 10. seguir 11. cantar 12. agarrar 13. viaje 14. navegar en internet 15. historias de ficción 16. seguir (haciendo) **Translate:** 1. por el[5] The island is surrounded by the Caribbean Sea. 2. dije[6] I've already told you that I am thirty-four years old. 3. en[16] I've been in that line of work for fifteen years. 4. ejerciendo[17] I hope I can continue to practice because it is something that I'm very passionate about. 5. el[24] When I go on a trip, the part I enjoy most is the journey, not getting there. 6. sea[30] I like to read books about any topic that is interesting.

Francisco

Francisco (Spain)
318 words (137 wpm)
5

True or False

1. Francisco is a DJ.   T ☐ F ☐
2. He worked as an actor both in theater and cinema.   T ☐ F ☐
3. He used to be a musician.   T ☐ F ☐
4. He likes watching sports but he dislikes doing them.   T ☐ F ☐
5. He cares about air pollution.   T ☐ F ☐

Expressions

¡Hasta luego!	both...and
¡Seguimos en contacto!	consisting of
desde hace mucho tiempo	for a long time
formado por	I'm into; I'm keen on
lo que más me gusta	if I can
montar en bicicleta	keep in touch!
mucho más que	much more than
no sólo	not only
si puedo	to ride a bike
soy aficionado a	trips
tanto...como	until then!
trayectos	what I like most

Multiple Choice

1. Francisco's daughter is __ years old.
    a. two   c. fourteen
    b. twelve   d. *none of the above*

2. Which of the following is <u>not</u> true about Francisco: he's married.
    a. He's married.
    b. He has a daughter named Andrea.
    c. He has a bicycle.
    d. He can't swim well.

3. In his free time, Francisco likes ___.
    a. shopping with his wife
    b. doing chores around the house
    c. going to the countryside
    d. practicing with his band

Text

¡Hola! Me llamo Francisco.	1	Hello! My name is Francisco.
Vivo en Madrid, la capital de España, y la ciudad en la que nací.	2	I live in Madrid, the capital of Spain, and the city where I was born.
Vivo aquí con mi familia, formada por mi esposa y mi hija de doce años, Andrea.	3	I live here with my family, consisting of my wife and my 12-year-old daughter, Andrea.
Trabajo desde hace mucho tiempo en el mundo del sonido y de la música,	4	I've been working in the world of sound and music for a long time,

donde he hecho mi carrera profesional,	5	where I've made my professional career,
tanto sonorizando programas de televisión, series, documentales, o anuncios, como poniendo música a programas como esos, y otros, cortometrajes, por ejemplo, y teatro también.	6	both doing sound for television programs, series, documentaries, or commercials, and music for programs like these, and others, short films, for example, and theater too.
Normalmente trabajo en mi estudio de producción casero,	7	Normally I work in my home production studio,
pero a veces también lo hago en emisoras de televisión, platós de cine o estudios de grabación profesionales.	8	but sometimes I do it at television stations, movie sets, or professional recording studios.
En el pasado hice música, grabando y tocando en directo con grupos musicales, algunos de los cuales, pues, llegamos a tener premios y todo.	9	In the past, I made music, recording and playing live with bands, some of which, well, we got awards and everything.
Pero desde hace unos años, me dedico principalmente a la composición de mis propias músicas en mi estudio,	10	But for a few years now, I've been concentrating on composing my own music in my studio,
que a la vez de ser una de mis mayores aficiones, me ayuda a completar mi vida profesional como compositor.	11	which, while also being one of my favorite hobbies, helps me fulfill my professional life as a composer.
Soy aficionado a practicar deporte—no sólo a verlo—sino también practicarlo.	12	I'm into doing sports—not just watching them—but also doing them.
Me gusta nadar, me gusta salir a correr, me gusta jugar al tenis o al paddle,	13	I like swimming; I like going running; I like playing tennis or paddle tennis,
pero lo que más me gusta es montar en bicicleta, no sólo por hacer deporte sino también por trasladarme.	14	but what I like most is riding bikes, not only for exercise but also to get around.
Cuando salgo de casa, eh... si puedo, me llevo la bicicleta y así hago trayectos por la ciudad en bici,	15	When I leave the house, uh... if I can, I take my bike and make trips around town by bike,
que se disfrutan mucho más que en coche o en transporte público.	16	which are much more enjoyable than by car or on public transportation.
Así que aprovecho cualquier trayecto urbano o por el campo para moverme en este vehículo tan sano y no contaminante.	17	So, I take any urban route or [route] through the country to get around with this healthy and non-contaminating vehicle.
Los fines de semana, cuando no trabajo, lo que más me gusta es salir al campo,	18	On weekends, when I'm not working, what I like most is to go to the countryside,
salir a darme buenas caminatas por fuera de Madrid, que tenemos unas montañas estupendas.	19	to go on some nice hikes outside of Madrid, as we have some great mountains.
Y poco más, ya os he contado quién soy, a qué me dedico, y un poco cuáles son mis aficiones.	20	That's about it. I've already told you who I am, what I do, and a bit about my interests.
¡Seguimos en contacto, hasta luego!	21	We'll be in touch! Until then!

Vocabulary

1. sound[4] _____
2. short film[6] _____
3. television stations[8] _____
4. movie sets[8] _____
5. recording studios[8] _____
6. band[9] _____
7. award[9] _____
8. my own[10] _____
9. hobby, passion[11] _____
10. to swim[13] _____
11. healthy[17] _____
12. non-contaminating[17] _____
13. countryside[18] _____
14. already[20] _____

Translate

1. Vivo aquí con mi familia, formada *para / por* mi esposa y mi hija de doce años.
2. Trabajo desde *hace / -* mucho tiempo.
3. En el pasado (yo) *hice / hizo* música, grabando y tocando en directo con grupos musicales.
4. Me gusta jugar *al / -* tenis.
5. Los trayectos en bicicleta se disfrutan mucho más *que / de* en coche o en transporte público.
6. Lo que me gusta es *- / a salir* al campo.

notes

True or False: 1. F[4] 2. F[6] 3. T[9] 4. F[12] 5. T[17] **Expressions:** ¡Hasta luego! - until then! / ¡Seguimos en contacto! - keep in touch! / desde hace mucho tiempo - for a long time / formado por - consisting of / lo que más me gusta - what I like most / montar en bicicleta - to ride a bike / mucho más que - much more than / no sólo - not only / si puedo - if I can / soy aficionado a - I'm into; I'm keen on / tanto...como - both...and / trayectos - trips **Multiple Choice:** 1. b[3] 2. d[13]. c[18] **Vocabulary:** 1. sonido 2. cortometraje 3. emisoras de televisión 4. platós de cine 5. estudios de grabación 6. grupo musical 7. premio 8. mi propio 9. afición 10. nadar 11. sano 12. no contaminante 13. campo 14. ya **Translate:** 1. para[3] I live here with my family, consisting of my wife and my twelve-year-old daughter. 2. hace[4] I have been working for a long time. 3. hice[9] In the past, I made music, recording and playing live with bands. 4. al[13] I like playing tennis. 5. que[16] Bicycle trips are much more enjoyable than by car or on public transportation. 6. -[19] What I like is to go to the countryside.

Florencia

Florencia (Argentina)
379 words (145 wpm)   6

True or False

1. Florencia is a housewife.   T ☐   F ☐
2. She stopped working when her first daughter was born.   T ☐   F ☐
3. She spends a lot of time at home.   T ☐   F ☐
4. In their free time, Florencia and her husband like going out.   T ☐   F ☐
5. She likes spending time on her own.   T ☐   F ☐

Expressions

entre	between
es lo que nos gusta hacer	I like spending time with friends
mantenerse al tanto	it is what we like to do.
me gusta pasar tiempo con amigos	most of all
o sea	that is
principalmente	to keep up with
somos buenos anfitriones	we're good hosts

Multiple Choice

1. After her daughter was born, Florencia ___.
   a. started her own business   c. quit her job
   b. had to find a new job   d. started working from home

2. According to tradition in Argentina, ___ at barbecue parties.
   a. men do all of the cooking while women relax
   b. children prepare the food while their parents relax
   c. women do all of the cooking while men relax
   d. men barbecue the meat while women make salads

3. A "canasta" is a party where ___.
   a. people play party games on teams
   b. everyone brings a dish to share
   c. children are taught to prepare food
   d. people get to know their new neighbors

Text

¡Hola! Mi nombre es Florencia.	1	Hello! My name is Florencia.
Eh… soy de Argentina.	2	Uh… I'm from Argentina.
Tengo cuarenta y un años.	3	I'm 41 years old.
Soy casada y tengo dos hijas.	4	I'm married, and I have two daughters.
Victoria, de dos años e Isabella, de cinco.	5	Victoria, two years old, and Isabella, five.
Estoy casada hace siete años y… tengo una familia hermosa.	6	I've been married for seven years and… I have a beautiful family.
Eh… lo que hago para ayudar en mi casa y trabajar,	7	Uh… what I do to help out at home and work,

em... soy asistente virtual, o sea, que trabajo desde casa.	8	um... I'm a virtual assistant; that is, I work from home.
Desde los dieciocho años hasta que nació mi primer hija trabajé en empresas internacionales, muy importantes,	9	From when I was 18 until my first daughter was born, I worked at very important international companies,
pero... cuando nació Isabella decidí... quedarme en casa para poder estar con ella.	10	but... when Isabella was born, I decided... to stay home to be with her.
Y... encontré la manera de encontrar un equilibrio entre... estar con la familia	11	and... I found a way to strike a balance between... being with my family
y también poder aportar económicamente en... en casa.	12	and also being able to contribute economically from... from home.
Así que puedo decir que soy afortunada de poder pasar tiempo en casa	13	So, I can say I'm lucky to be able to spend time at home
pero sin dejar el mundo laboral, sin dejar el mundo profesional,	14	without leaving the working world, without leaving the professional world,
para poder siempre estar, eh... informada y siempre poder estar... mantenerme al tanto de lo que sucede en el mundo.	15	to always be, uh... informed and always be able to be... to keep up with what is happening in the [outside] world.
Lo que más me gusta hacer es em... poder salir con mi esposo.	16	What I like to do the most is, um... is to go out with my husband.
A nosotros nos gusta mucho salir a comer, probar distintas comidas.	17	We really like going out to eat, try different [kinds of] food.
Nos gusta mucho ir al cine.	18	We like going to the movies a lot.
Básicamente cualquier cosa que... que... no implique niños dando vueltas y teniendo interrupciones es lo que más nos gusta hacer.	19	Basically, anything that... that... does not involve children running around and interrupting us is what we like to do most.
Eh... también nos gusta mucho recibir amigos.	20	Uh... we also love having friends over.
Somos muy buenos anfitriones.	21	We are very good hosts.
Usualmente en Argentina los amigos se juntan para comer un asado... que es comer, eh... tirar carne en la parrilla.	22	Usually, in Argentina, friends gather for a barbecue... that is to eat, uh... throw meat on the grill.
Y... en general son los hombres que hacen el asado y las mujeres hacemos las ensaladas.	23	And... generally, men do the barbecuing, and we women make the salads.
Así que mientras ellos conversan por su lado, nosotras conversamos mientras hacemos las ensaladas y después nos juntamos todos.	24	So while they chat amongst themselves, we [women] talk while we make the salads, and then we all come together.
En los momentos más difíciles donde no hay tanta plata hacemos algo "a la canasta".	25	In the most difficult moments when there is not too much money, we do something called "a la canasta."
Eh... "a la canasta" quiere decir que cada uno trae algo, trae algo para comer.	26	Uh... "a la canasta" means that everyone brings something, brings something to eat.
Lo ponemos en la mesa y lo compartimos.	27	We put it on the table and share it.
Entonces bueno, todos dividimos los gastos de esa manera.	28	So, well, all expenses are divided that way.
Así que, eh... diría yo que eh... pasar tiempo con amigos, pasar tiempo en familia...	29	So, uh... I would say that uh... spending time with friends, spending time with family...

una buena charla, una buena conversación, una buena comida, un buen tiempo… pasarla bien es lo que, lo que más me gusta.	a good chat, good conversation, good food, a good time… having a good time is what, what I like.
Y principalmente la paso bien cuando estoy en compañía de mis amigos y de mi familia.	And most of all I have a good time when I'm in the company of my friends and my family.
Eso es un poco lo que… lo que me define.	That's kinda what… what defines me.

Vocabulary

1. to be born[10] _____
2. balance[11] _____
3. to contribute[12] _____
4. host[21] _____
5. grill[22] _____
6. to gather[22] _____
7. meat[22] _____
8. barbecue[23] _____
9. money[25] _____
10. to share[27] _____
11. table[27] _____
12. expenses[28] _____
13. chat[30] _____
14. to have a good time[30] _____

Translate

1. Tengo una hija *de / tiene* dos años.
2. Lo hago para mantenerme *al tanto / al lado* de lo que pasa en el mundo.
3. A nosotros *nos gusta / gustamos* ir al cine.
4. Los amigos se *juntan / huntan* para comer un asado.
5. Cada uno trae algo *para / por* comer.
6. Cuando *estoy / soy* en compañía de mis amigos siempre la paso bien.

notes

True or False: 1. F[8] 2. F[9] 3. T[13] 4. T[17] 5. F[31] **Expressions:** entre - between / es lo que nos gusta hacer - it is what we like to do. / mantenerse al tanto - to keep up with / me gusta pasar tiempo con amigos - I like spending time with friends / o sea - that is / principalmente - most of all / somos buenos anfitriones. - we're good hosts / **Multiple Choice:** 1. d[13-14] 2. d[23] 3. b[26] **Vocabulary:** 1. nacer 2. equilibrio 3. aportar 4. anfitrión 5. parrilla 6. juntarse 7. carne 8. asado 9. plata 10. compartir 11. mesa 12. gastos 13. charla 14. pasarla bien **Translate:** 1. de[5] I have a two-year-old daughter. 2. al tanto[15] I do it to keep up with what is happening in the world. 3. nos gusta[18] We like to go to the movies. 4. juntan[22] Friends gather to have barbecue. 5. para[26] Everyone brings something to eat. 6. estoy[31] When I am in the company of my friends, I always have a good time.

Rutinas Diarias

La Rutina Diaria de Laura

Laura (Costa Rica)
428 words (125 wpm) 7

True or False

1. Laura gets up late in the morning.   T☐ F☐
2. Laura almost never has dogs to take care of.   T☐ F☐
3. Laura usually takes her children to school.   T☐ F☐
4. When her kids go to school, Laura drives to her office.   T☐ F☐
5. Laura's husband picks up the children from school.   T☐ F☐

Expressions

a veces	after
cenamos	again
cualquier cosa	every day
de nuevo	I come home
después de	I don't know
en eso me tomo cinco minutos	I go back home
llego a la casa	I pick them up
los recojo	in the meantime
más o menos	it takes me five minutes
mientras tanto	more or less
no sé	of course
por supuesto	once
regreso a casa	sometimes
todos los días	we have dinner
una vez que	whatever

Multiple Choice

1. How might Laura describe her typical day?

    a. boring   b. easy   c. stressful   d. busy

2. When Laura gets up, the first thing she does is ___.

    a. check her email   c. walk the dogs
    b. make coffee   d. take the kids to school

3. What does Laura sometimes do in the evening after dinner?

    a. go to the supermarket   c. go to fitness class
    b. check her work email   d. *all of the above*

Text

Bueno, mi rutina diaria:	1	Well, my daily routine:
Todos los días me levanto a las seis de la mañana.	2	I wake up at 6 a.m. every morning.
A esa hora tengo el despertador.	3	My alarm is set for this time.
Y me levanto a las seis.	4	And I wake up at six.
Y lo primero que hago es: ¡hacer café! Por supuesto.	5	And the first thing I do is: make coffee! Of course.
Entonces, pongo el coffee maker a hacer café,	6	So, I turn on the coffee maker,
y mientras tanto, eh... cuando tengo perritos, que es casi todos los días que me los dejan,	7	and while [the coffee is being made], uh... if I have doggies, which is almost every day that they leave them with me,
entonces saco a los perritos a que hagan pipí.	8	then I take the dogs out to have a pee.
Entonces en eso me tomo unos quince - veinte minutos,	9	This takes me 15-20 minutes
porque les doy la vuelta por toda la calle,	10	because we go all the way down the street
y hacen sus cositas los perritos.	11	so that they can take care of their business.
Y ya llego a la casa,	12	And then I get back to the house,
me sirvo el café,	13	I get myself my coffee,
y me pongo a alistar a los chicos porque tienen que ir a la escuela.	14	and I start getting the kids ready because they have to go to school.
Entran a las ocho.	15	They start at eight.
Entonces ya despertarlos, que se vayan levantando,	16	So [I] wake them up, so they'll get up,
les hago el desayuno—	17	I make them breakfast—
casi siempre comen huevos con jamón o corn flakes.	18	they usually have eggs and ham or some corn flakes.
Entonces bueno, les doy el desayuno, se alistan.	19	Then they finish their breakfast,
Les ayudo un poco porque a veces son medios perezosos.	20	and I kind of [have to] help them because they can be a little lazy sometimes.
Y mi esposo también mientras tanto se alista.	21	At the same time, my husband is getting ready too.
Él también desayuna y todos se van como tropa a las ocho y me quedo sola.	22	He has some breakfast too, and they all head out like a troop at eight, and I'm left alone.
Una vez que estoy sola en casa, ya con calma y después de la carrera de la mañana, me pongo a trabajar.	23	Once I am alone in the house, nice and quiet, after all of the running around in the morning, I get to work.
Así que reviso mi correo, cuáles son las traducciones, mis tareas que hacer,	24	I check my email [to see] which are my daily translations, my to-do list,
las hago casi siempre por ahí del medio día ya terminé, una de la tarde ya.	25	and I finish around noon or 1 p.m.
Me hago algo de comer.	26	I make myself something to eat.
No sé, cualquier cosa, una ensalada, ahí yo...casi no almuerzo mucho.	27	I don't know, just whatever, a salad. I usually don't eat much for lunch.

Saco de nuevo a los perritos.	28	I go out again with the dogs.
Esta vez si los camino más—una hora por ahí.	29	This time is a longer walk—one hour maybe.
Caminamos, salimos, vamos al parque.	30	We walk, go out, go to the park.
Después regreso a casa, casi ya es hora de ir a recoger a los chicos a la escuela.	31	Then I go back home, [because] it is almost time to go pick up the kids from school.
Los recojo. Ellos vienen.	32	I pick them up. They come [home].
En la tarde, hacemos las tareas.	33	In the afternoons, we do homework.
Me dedico también a alguna cosa—siempre hay algo que hacer,	34	I also spend time doing something—there is always something to do,
o llamadas de teléfono, o tengo que ensayar, no sé, siempre hay algo.	35	phone calls, or I have to rehearse, I don't know, there's always something.
O hay alguna cita al doctor, no sé, ir al correo, buscar algo, ir al súper.	36	Or there is some doctor's appointment; I don't know, going to the post office, looking for something, going to the supermarket.
Ya mi esposo llega como a las seis, siete por ahí y cenamos.	37	My husband arrives around six or seven, and we have dinner.
Casi siempre después de cenar también salgo de nuevo a caminar a los perros, otros 45 minutos -1 hora más o menos.	38	After dinner, I almost always go out to walk the dogs again, another 45 minutes - 1 hour or so.
Y también a veces en las noches, me gusta, a veces hay… voy a Zumba o hay clases de alguna cosa,	39	And also in the evening, there are sometimes… I like to… I go to Zumba classes, or whatever classes,
entonces voy, o tengo ensayo.	40	so I go, or I have [theater] rehearsal.
Y básicamente ese es un día digamos que normal en mi vida.	41	Basically, that's a, shall we say, regular day in my life.
Hay veces que son días locos,	42	Some days are really crazy,
pero esto más o menos es un día tranquilo.	43	but this is a very normal one.

Vocabulary

1. to get up[2] _____
2. alarm[3] _____
3. first[5] _____
4. almost[7] _____
5. to get ready[14] _____
6. to wake up[16] _____
7. lazy[20] _____
8. alone[22] _____
9. to check[24] _____
10. something[26] _____
11. to have lunch[27] _____
12. afternoon[33] _____
13. phone calls[35] _____
14. appointment[36] _____
15. regular[41] _____

Translate

1. Me levanto a las seis *de / en* la mañana.
2. Ayudo a los chicos *porque / para que* tienen que ir a la escuela.
3. Ellos comen h*uevos / juevos*.
4. *Me pongo a / Pongo de trabajar a las ocho.*
5. Todos los días *recojo / recogo* a los chicos a las cuatro.

6. Después *de cenar / la cena*, salgo.

notes

True or False: 1. F[2] 2. F[7] 3. F[22] 4. F[23] 5. F[32] **Expressions:** a veces - sometimes / cenamos - we have dinner / cualquier cosa - whatever / de nuevo - again / después de - after / en eso me tomo cinco minutos - it takes me five minutes / llego a la casa - I come home / los recojo - I pick them up / más o menos - more or less / mientras tanto - in the meantime / no sé - I don't know / por supuesto - of course / regreso a casa - I go back home. / todos los días - every day / una vez que - once / **Multiple Choice:** 1. d 2. b[5] 3. c[39] **Vocabulary:** 1. levantarse 2. despertador 3. primero 4. casi 5. alistar 6. despertar(se) 7. perezoso 8. sola 9. revisar 10. algo 11. almorzar 12. tarde 13. llamadas de teléfono 14. cita 15. Normal **Translate:** 1. de[2] I wake up at six in the morning. 2. porque[14] I help the kids/boys because they have to go to school. 3. huevos[18] They eat eggs. 4. me pongo a[23] I start working at eight. 5. recojo[31] Every day, I pick up the kids/boys at four (o'clock). 6. de cenar[38] After dinner, I go out.

La Rutina Diaria de Jorge

Jorge (Peru)
391 words (125 wpm)
8

True or False

1. Lately Jorge doesn't have a lot of work to do. T☐ F☐
2. In Peru, on Tuesday, movie tickets are on sale. T☐ F☐
3. Jorge plays in a rock band. T☐ F☐
4. Jorge likes to go dancing. T☐ F☐
5. Jorge, typical of a South American person, is very good at dancing. T☐ F☐

Expressions

al igual que	as, like
bastante variedad	between
distraído	distracted
entre	I'm a homebody
soy una persona de casa	quite a variety
tres veces por semana	three times a week

Multiple Choice

1. In the morning, Jorge prefers ___.
   a. skipping breakfast   c. eating a hearty breakfast
   b. eating very little   d. He doesn't mention anything about this.

2. Cinema is also called ___.
   a. the silver television   c. the theater of light
   b. the seventh art   d. talking stories

3. Jorge's favorite genre of music is ___.
   a. jazz   c. rock
   b. folk   d. none of the above

Text

Un día normal para mi es levantarme entre siete y ocho de la mañana,	1	A normal day for me is to get up between seven and eight a.m.,
si el cuerpo me lo permite ahora que estoy desempleado,	2	if my body allows me now that I'm unemployed,
y que no estoy haciendo mucho por el momento.	3	and I'm not doing much at the moment.
Eh... tengo una nueva rutina de vida.	4	Uh... I have a new routine in life.
Me gusta... me gusta mantenerme activo.	5	I like... I like to keep active.
Siempre he sido una persona activa.	6	I have always been an active person.
Eh... voy al gimnasio tres veces por semana ahora.	7	Uh... I go to the gym three times a week now.
Me gusta comenzar el día con un buen desayuno,	8	I like to start the day with a good breakfast,

cosa de que así tengo energía… mucha, mucha energía durante el resto del día.	9	which I thus get energy from… lots and lots of energy for the rest of the day.
Em… soy una persona muy… muy de casa.	10	Um… I am quite… quite a homebody.
Me gusta estar en casa. Eh… bueno, la comodidad, bueno, de mi cuarto.	11	I like to be at home. Uh… well, the comfort, well, of my room.
Tengo suerte de tener muchas cosas electrónicas que me tienen muy distraído.	12	I'm lucky to have many electronic things that keep me very distracted.
Me encantan las series; es algo que me gusta hacer en mis ratos de ocio.	13	I love series. It's something I like to do in my leisure time.
Eh… bueno, si no estoy en casa, siempre me gusta estar con mis amigos.	14	Uh… well, if I'm not home, I always like to be with my friends.
Eh… normalmente los martes acá, creo al igual que em… en el resto del mundo, es el día del cine—es como dos por uno.	15	Uh… usually on Tuesdays here, I think as um… in the rest of the world, it's movie day—it's like two for one.
Soy alguien que está… bueno, que tiene mucha afición por el séptimo arte.	16*	I am someone who is… well, that has a great liking for the seventh art.
Em… los fines de semana es algo que espero siempre al inicio de toda semana,	17	Um… weekends are something I always look forward to at the beginning of every week,
porque así eh… bueno soy una persona muy social.	18	because uh… well, I am a very social person.
Me gusta salir con mis amigos.	19	I like hanging out with my friends.
Eh… soy alguien que disfruta mucho de la música.	20	Uh… I'm someone who really enjoys music.
Tengo un aspecto un poco rockero,	21	I have a bit of a rocker look,
pero irónicamente no toco ningún tipo instrumento,	22	but ironically I don't play any kind of instrument,
a comparación de todos mis amigos, que son músicos ¿eh?	23	as opposed to all my friends, who are musicians, yeah?
Un poco irónico ¿no? de la vida.	24	A little ironic of life, right?
Eh… me gusta la música de los noventas.	25	Uh… I like 90s music.
Soy un chico de los noventas—sí me gusta… me gusta el rock.	26	I'm a 90s guy, and I like, I like rock.
Em… en Lima hay bastante variedad de… de clubes, no en ese sentido, ¿no? Hay para todo tipo de… todo tipo de gusto.	27	Um… in Lima, there is quite a variety of clubs, not in that sense, okay? There's [something] for all kinds of taste.
A veces si es que se da la oportunidad, me gusta salir a bailar también.	28	Sometimes if given the opportunity, I like to go out and dance, too.
Poco raro para un chico que le gusta el rock, ¿no?	29	A little weird for a guy who likes rock, right?
Acá, bueno, como es Sudamérica eh… la salsa es muy popular, ¿no?	30	Here, well, as it's South America uh… salsa is really popular, yeah?
Eso que dicen de que todo… toda persona latina tiene oi-… oído para la música,	31	That thing they say—that every… every Latin person has an ea-… ear for music,
y bailan naturalmente porque está escrito en su genética,	32	and they dance naturally because it is written in their genes—
es… no se aplica a todo los casos.	33	it's… it isn't applicable in all cases.

Yo soy uno de ellos porque mi coordinación es muy mala.	34	I am one of these [cases] because my coordination is very bad.
Disfruto la música. Eh... me entra por el oído pero no coordino nada bien.	35	I enjoy music. Uh... it goes in my ears, but I'm not coordinated at all.

***16** Since ancient times, the artistic disciplines have been categorized as architecture, sculpture, painting, music, dance, and poetry. With the advent of cinema, Riccioto Canudo, an Italian poet and film critic, coined the term 'the seventh art' to include it among the classical artistic disciplines.

Vocabulary

1. unemployed[2] _____
2. routine[4] _____
3. comfort[11] _____
4. luck[12] _____
5. leisure time[13] _____
6. here[15] _____
7. fondness, liking[16] _____
8. to play an instrument[22] _____
9. sometimes[28] _____
10. weird, odd[29] _____

Translate

1. Un día normal para mi es *levantarme / me levanto* entre siete y ocho de la mañana.
2. Voy al gimnasio tres veces *por / per* semana ahora.
3. Tengo suerte *de / a* tener muchas cosas electrónicas que me tienen muy distraído.
4. Me gusta la música de *los / las* noventas.
5. Me gusta salir *a / -* bailar.
6. Disfruto *- / de* la música.

notes

True or False: 1. T[3] 2. T[15] 3. F[22] 4. T[28] 5. F[34] **Expressions:** al igual que - as, like / bastante variedad - quite a variety / distraído - distracted / entre - between / soy una persona de casa - I'm a homebody / tres veces por semana - three times a week **Multiple Choice:** 1. a[8-9] 2. b[16] 3. c[26] **Vocabulary:** 1. desempleado 2. rutina 3. comodidad 4. suerte 5. ratos de ocio 6. acá 7. afición 8. tocar un instrumento 9. a veces 10. raro **Translate:** 1. levantarme[1] A normal day for me is to get up between seven and eight in the morning. 2. por[7] I go to the gym three times a week now. 3. de[12] I'm lucky to have many electronic things that keep me very distracted. 4. los[25] I like 90s music. 5. a[28] I like to go out to dance. 6. -[35] I enjoy music.

La Rutina Diaria de Sandra

Sandra (Mexico)
384 words (128 wpm)
9

True or False

1. Sandra takes her son to preschool and then goes to her office. T ☐ F ☐
2. Sandra and her son wait for her husband to come back from work before having lunch. T ☐ F ☐
3. Sandra works both in the morning and in the afternoon. T ☐ F ☐
4. Sandra and her husband have lunch together but not dinner. T ☐ F ☐
5. After dinner, Sandra goes for a walk. T ☐ F ☐

Expressions

a eso de	
alrededor de	a little bit more
apenas	again
casi siempre	almost always
de esta forma	around (2x)
entre	between
lo primero que hago	I go to sleep
me voy a dormir	not yet
otra vez	only
por lo regular	the first thing I do
todavía no	this way
un poco más	usually

Multiple Choice

1. Sandra gets up at __.

   a. 5:30   c. 7:30
   b. 6:00   d. *none of the above*

2. The first thing Sandra does when she wakes up is ___.

   a. have a cup of coffee   c. take a shower
   b. cook breakfast for her husband   d. wake up her son

3. What does Sandra do around eight o'clock in the evening?

   a. She gets her son ready for bed.   c. She reads or watches TV in bed.
   b. She cooks dinner for her family.   d. She makes sure the front door is locked.

Text

Por lo regular me levanto a las siete y media.	1	I usually wake up at half-past six.
Y lo primero que hago es meterme a bañar.	2	And the first thing I do is take a shower.
De esta forma me siento un poco más despierta.	3	This way, I feel a little bit more awake.
Después de bañarme preparo el desayuno.	4	After taking a shower, I make breakfast.
Y... como a eso de las ocho y media levanto a mi hijo y desayunamos juntos.	5	And... around half-past eight, I wake my son up, and we have breakfast together.
Mi hijo todavía no va a la escuela; tiene apenas tres años.	6	My son doesn't go to school yet; he's only three years old.
Eh... yo trabajo desde casa; entonces alrededor de las nueve me pongo a trabajar.	7	Uh... I work from home, so around nine, I start working.
Trabajo de nueve a doce aproximadamente,	8	I work from nine to twelve approximately,
y después, después de trabajar, después de las doce, me pongo a hacer em... mis tareas en la casa.	9	and then, after working, after twelve, I start doing um... my chores around the house.
Me pongo a limpiar la casa, hacer un poco de quehacer.	10	I start cleaning the house, do a little bit of housework,
Em... ya después como a eso de las doce y media me pongo a hacer la comida.	11	Um... after that, around half-past twelve, I start making lunch.
Y mi hijo y yo comemos juntos alrededor de la una o la una y media.	12	And my son and I eat together around one or half-past one.
No tenemos una hora precisa, pero entre una o una y media comemos.	13	We don't have a specific time, but between one or half-past one we eat;
Después de comer juego un poco con mi hijo.	14	After eating, I play with my son a little.
Estoy un rato con él, jugamos.	15	I spend some time with him; we play.
Y después, después de la comida como alrededor de las tres me pongo a trabajar otra vez.	16	And then, after lunch, like around... three, I get back to work.
Trabajo por... por otras dos horas, aproximadamente, de tres a cinco trabajo otra vez.	17	I work for... for another two hours approximately, from three to five I work again.
Y después de terminar de trabajar me pongo a preparar la cena.	18	And after I finish working, I start making dinner,
Esto es alrededor de las seis.	19	This is around six.
Luego mi esposo llega a casa alrededor de las seis y media,	20	Then my husband comes home around half-past six,
y entonces cenamos todos juntos a las seis y media casi siempre.	21	and then we have dinner all together at half-past six, almost always.
Después de la cena lo que regularmente—no todos los días pero regularmente—yo salgo a caminar. Me gusta... me gusta caminar.	22	After dinner, what I usually—not every day but usually—I go out for a walk. I like... I like walking.
Después... después de cenar y ya cuando... cuando regreso de caminar, que son como las ocho cuando... cuando regreso, eh... empiezo a preparar a mi hijo para... para ir a la cama.	23	Then, after dinner and when... when I come back from walking, which is around eight when... when I come back, uh... I start getting my son ready for... to go to bed.

Lo baño, le pongo su pijama y le leo un cuento.	24	I bathe him, I put his pajamas on, and I read him a story.
Aproximadamente como ocho y media mi hijo se... se duerme.	25	Approximately around half past eight, my son... falls asleep.
Y entonces ya yo tengo tiempo para... para hacer mis cosas.	26	And then I have time to... to do my things.
Em... regularmente lo que... lo que hago después de poner a mi hijo en... en la cama es:	27	Um... what I usually... what I usually do after putting my son in... in bed is:
me pongo... me pongo a ver la tele o me pongo a leer algún libro.	28	I... I watch TV, or I read a book.
Ya tengo más tiempo para mi.	29	I have more time for myself.
Y finalmente me voy a dormir alrededor de las once o las once y media.	30	And I finally go to sleep around eleven or half-past eleven.

Vocabulary

1. housework[10] _____
2. to clean the house[10] _____
3. to start to[11] _____
4. together[12] _____
5. a moment[15] _____
6. to make dinner[18] _____
7. usually[22] _____
8. to fall asleep[25] _____
9. TV[28] _____
10. time for myself[29] _____

Translate

1. *Por / En* lo regular me levanto temprano.
2. *De / En* esta forma me siento un poco más despierta.
3. Trabajo *por / para* otras dos horas, aproximadamente.
4. Alrededor *de / -* las seis me pongo a preparar la cena.
5. Mi esposo llega *a / en* casa alrededor de las seis y media.
6. *Cenamos / Cenemos* todos juntos a las seis y media casi siempre.

notes

True or False: 1. F[7] 2. F[13] 3. T[16] 4. F[21] 5. T[22] **Expressions:** a eso de - around / alrededor de - around / apenas - only / casi siempre - almost always / de esta forma - this way / entre - between / lo primero que hago - the first thing I do / me voy a dormir - I go to sleep / otra vez - again / por lo regular - usually / todavía no - not yet / un poco más - a little bit more **Multiple Choice:** 1. d[1] 2. c[2] 3. a[23] **Vocabulary:** 1. quehacer 2. limpiar la casa 3. ponerse a 4. juntos 5. un rato 6. preparar la cena 7. regularmente 8. dormirse 9. tele 10. tiempo para mi **Translate:** 1. por[1] I usually get up early. 2. de[3] This way, I feel a little more awake. 3. por[17] I work for about another two hours. 4. de[18] Around six, I start preparing dinner. 5. a[20] My husband arrives home around six-thirty. 6. cenamos[21] We almost always all have dinner together at six-thirty.

La Rutina Diaria de José

José (Honduras)
407 words (154 wpm) 🔊 10

True or False

1. José's wife gets up a little earlier than him in order to get the children ready. T ☐ F ☐
2. Jose's wife takes the children to school because she works in the school they attend. T ☐ F ☐
3. José works until 6:30 p.m. T ☐ F ☐
4. In the afternoon José has to take his children to the gym. T ☐ F ☐
5. All of Jose's children sleep in the same room. T ☐ F ☐

Expressions

a la misma hora	a bit
a través de	as I said
al menos	at least
como les decía	at the same time
hasta	early
o sea que	so-then
por lo tanto	through
temprano	until
un poco	which means

Multiple Choice

1. Which of the following is true?
    a. He has lunch at work.
    b. He has lunch at home after work.
    c. He comes home for lunch then goes back to work.
    d. He often skips lunch because he's too busy.

2. What does José like to do in the afternoon?
    a. watch television
    b. go for a jog
    c. work on his motorcycle
    d. read the newspaper

3. Before José's children go to bed, José ___.
    a. tells them a bedtime story
    b. lets them watch a cartoon on YouTube
    c. reads the Bible with them
    d. teaches them some English words

Text

Mi rutina diaria.	1	My daily routine.
Pues, me levanto temprano a las cinco de la mañana.	2	Well, I get up early at five in the morning.
A esa hora tengo que levantar a los niños para ayudarles a bañarse, a vestirse, para ir a la escuela.	3	That's when I have to get the children up and help them take their baths and get dressed to go to school.

Mi esposa también se levanta a la misma hora.	4	My wife also gets up at the same time.
Ella también sale a trabajar.	5	She goes to work, too.
Usualmente levanto a los niños, los mando a desayunar.	6	I usually make the kids get up and tell them to go eat breakfast.
Ellos desayunan cereal, algún pan con margarina o jalea, o tal vez panqueques, dependiendo del tiempo.	7	For breakfast, they usually have cereal, some bread with margarine or jelly, or maybe pancakes, depending on the [amount of] time [available].
Yo trabajo en una escuela, que es escuela, es prescolar, y también es secundaria.	8	I work in a school, which is a school, a preschool, and also a high school.
Mis niños: uno está en prescolar, el otro está en la escuela.	9	My children: one is in preschool, the other is in school.
Él se queda en la casa.	10	He stays at home.
Pues, nos alistamos para ir a la escuela.	11	So, we get ready to go to school.
Ellos, los niños, como les decía, ellos van a la misma escuela donde yo trabajo,	12	They, the children, as I said, they go to the same school where I work,
o sea que yo me los llevo.	13	which means I take them with me.
Mi esposa se va al instituto donde ella trabaja, porque ella también es docente.	14	My wife goes to the institute where she works because she is also a teacher.
Y pues llego al trabajo.	15	And then I arrive at work.
Estoy em... ahí de seis y media hasta las dos treinta de la tarde.	16	I am um... there from 6:30 until 2:30 p.m.
A esa hora, pues, regreso a casa.	17	At that time, then, I go back home.
Almuerzo a esa hora usualmente.	18	I usually have lunch at that time.
Sé que es un poco tarde pero por el trabajo prefiero mejor almorzar a esa hora: a las dos treinta - tres de la tarde.	19	I know it's a little late, but because of work, I prefer eating lunch at that time, 2:30 or 3 p.m.
Mis hijos llegan a las dos.	20	My children get home at 2:00.
El más pequeño, que está en prescolar, llega a las doce, por lo tanto él almuerza a esa hora.	21	The youngest, who is in preschool, gets home at 12, so he has lunch at that time.
Mi hijo, el otro, almuerza a las una y media - dos de la tarde.	22	My son, the other one, has lunch at 1:30 or 2 p.m.
Yo llego después a almorzar a las dos treinta.	23	Then I get home and have lunch at 2:30.
Y bueno, descanso un poco en la tarde.	24	And well, I rest a bit in the afternoon.
Luego me pongo a hacer algún trabajo del colegio,	25	Then I start to do some work for school,
algún papel que tenga que revisar, algún trabajo que tenga que investigar.	26	some documents I have to check, some work that I have to research.
A veces, lo que hago es... en la tarde, es ponerme a ver alguna película.	27	Sometimes, what I do is... in the afternoon, is to watch a movie.
Me gusta mucho ver películas.	28	I love watching movies.
Si hay deportes, veo los deportes.	29	If sports are on, I watch sports.
Me gusta también ver series a través de Netflix.	30	I also like to watch series through Netflix.
Y eso básicamente es mi rutina diaria.	31	And that's basically my daily routine.

Ya después en la tarde alistamos a los niños, ya como a las siete y media - ocho,	32	And then in the evening, we get the children ready, around 7:30 or 8:00,	
porque tienen que levantarse temprano para el día siguiente.	33	because they have to get up early the next day.	
Los vamos a bañar; los alistamos.	34	We go give them their baths and get them ready.	
Los tres duermen en el mismo cuarto.	35	All three sleep in the same room.	
Nos sentamos, les contamos historias.	36	We sit and tell them stories.	
Al menos yo me siento con ellos.	37	At least, I sit with them.	
Yo les cuento una historia antes de irse a dormir.	38	I tell them a story before they go to sleep.	
Los arropamos y luego, pues, ya tipo nueve y media - diez, yo pues me voy a dormir,	39	We tuck them in, and then, around 9:30 or 10, I, well, go to bed,	
a comenzar la jornada del día siguiente.	40	in order to start the next day.	

Vocabulary

1. to take a bath[3] _____
2. to get dressed[3] _____
3. bread[7] _____
4. jelly[7] _____
5. pancakes[7] _____
6. preschool[9] _____
7. to go back home[17] _____
8. the youngest[21] _____
9. to rest[24] _____
10. school[25] _____
11. to start doing[25] _____
12. to check[26] _____
13. the next day[33] _____
14. to tuck (someone) in[39] _____

Translate

1. A esa hora tengo que levantar a los niños para *ayudarles / ayudar* a bañarse, a vestirse, para ir a la escuela.
2. Ellos desayunan - */ de* cereal, algún pan con margarina o jalea, o tal vez panqueques.
3. Él se queda *en / a* la casa.
4. Luego me *pongo / empiezo* a hacer algún trabajo.
5. Ellos *tienen / deben* que levantarse temprano para el día siguiente.
6. Ellos duermen en *el / lo* mismo cuarto.

notes

True or False: 1. F[4] 2. F[16] 3. F[18] 4. F[25] 5. T[35] **Expressions:** a la misma hora - at the same time / a través de - through / al menos - at least / como les decía - as I said / hasta - until / o sea que - which means / por lo tanto - so-then / temprano - early / un poco - a bit / **Multiple Choice:** 1. b[19] 2. a[27-30] 3. a[36-38] **Vocabulary:** 1. whole[7] 2. grade[10] 3. to tell[16] 4. job[18] 5. time[36] 6. to take care of[40] 7. turtle[43] 8. to listen[45] **Translate:** 1. ayudarles[3] At that time, I have to get the kids up to help them bathe and get dressed to go to school. 2. -[7] They have breakfast cereal, some bread with margarine or jelly, or maybe pancakes. 3. en[10] He stays at home. 4. pongo[25] Then I start doing some work. 5. tienen[33] They have to get up early the next day. 6. el[35] They sleep in the same room.

Recuerdos de la Infancia

El Cometa

Laura (Costa Rica)
310 words (164 wpm) 🔊 11

True or False

1. That night Laura didn't get any sleep.   T☐ F☐
2. She went to the beach in order to observe the sky.   T☐ F☐
3. That night the sky was very cloudy.   T☐ F☐
4. She couldn't see anything through the binoculars.   T☐ F☐
5. She has a bad memory of that night.   T☐ F☐

Expressions

¿por qué?	ever again
¿Qué está pasando?	maybe
acaso	not anymore
claro	of course
de repente	so
entonces	suddenly
nunca mas	What's going on?
ya no	why?

Multiple Choice

1. Laura tells us about a time she ___.
   a. saw a comet
   b. learned about astronomy in school
   c. had a dream about space travel
   d. *none of the above*

2. Laura went to the beach with her ___.
   a. uncle
   b. father
   c. grandfather
   d. brother

3. Which of the following is true?
   a. The beach was 80 kilometers away.
   b. Laura's grandfather was 80 years old.
   c. The comet is only visible once every 80 years.
   d. Renting binoculars cost 80 CRC.

Text

Bueno, este recuerdo yo tenía si acaso unos, no sé, ocho, nueve años.	1	Well, this memory, I was maybe around, I don't know, eight, nine years old.
¡Y es cuando pasó el famoso cometa Halley!	2	And it's when the famous Halley's Comet was around!
Bueno, esto... no sé, yo poco recuerdo como de esa época,	3	Well, I don't know, I don't remember a lot from that age,

pero esto es algo que sí,	4	but this is something that I do
porque me recuerdo que mi papá me decía:	5	because I remember what my father said to me:
"Laura, grábese esto bien en la mente porque esto es algo que solamente una vez en la vida va a ver,	6*	Laura, engrave this in your memory because this is something you'll only see once in your lifetime
porque este cometa va a pasar hasta dentro de ochenta años	7	because this comet is going to appear again in about 80 years,
y usted ya seguramente no va a existir.	8	and you probably won't be around [then].
Entonces claro yo empecé a grabar todo en mi mente.	9	So, of course, I started to record everything in my mind.
Y eran como las tres de la mañana, me acuerdo que yo estaba requeté-dormida,	10*	It was about three in the morning, and I remember I was fast asleep,
y en eso me despierta mi papá.	11	and then my dad woke me up.
Estábamos en la playa,	12	We were at the beach,
y me dice: Laura, vamos a la playa, vamos, que le tengo que enseñar algo.	13	and he said, "Laura, let's go to the beach. Come on. I have something to show you."
Y entonces yo, claro, yo media dormida, abro los ojos	14	And then, of course, half asleep, I open my eyes,
y digo: ¿Qué está pasando? Es la madrugada, ¿por qué me están despertando?	15	and ask myself, "What's going on? It's so early. Why are you waking me up?
Y… y mi papá me puso una cobija en la espalda y me llevó a la playa, con unos binoculares.	16	Then… then my dad put a blanket on my shoulders and took me to the beach with a pair of binoculars.
Y me dijo: Vamos a ver un cometa que solamente pasa una vez cada ochenta años,	17	and he said to me, "We are going to see a comet that only appears every 80 years,
y esto usted nunca más lo va a volver a ver.	18	and you are not going to see it ever again."
Entonces me recuerdo que estábamos viendo, sentados en la arena, viendo aquel cielo, súper estrellado,	19	So, I remember that we were looking, sitting on the sand, looking at that starry sky
y él con los binoculares buscándolo… y lo encontró!	20	and him looking with the binoculars… and then he found it!
Me hace: ¡¡Ahí está, Laura, ahí está!!	21	He goes, "There it is, Laura, there it is!!"
Y me recuerdo que me puso los binoculares	22	And I remember that he gave me the binoculars,
y yo buscaba ¡y de repente lo vi! Lo vi con los binoculares,	23	and I looked for it, and suddenly I saw it! I saw it through the binoculars,
y le decía a mi papá: ¿Papi, pero qué es eso?	24	and I said to my dad, "But what is it?"
Entonces, él ya me explicaba que era un cometa,	25	So, he explained to me that it was a comet,
y me decía: Vele la colita; los cometas tienen colita.	26	and he kept saying, "Look at its little tail; comets have tails."
Y bueno, fue un momento muy lindo.	27	And, well, that was a really wonderful moment.
Fue precioso compartir con él y ver sentados en la playa el cometa Halley.	28	It was priceless sharing that with him, sitting on the beach, looking the Halley's Comet.

*6 In Costa Rica, usted (and its conjugations) is used instead of tú as the predominant pronoun for both formal and informal address.

*10 *requeté-* is a colloquial prefix that intensifies the adjective it precedes, synonymous with *súper* or *-ísimo*.

Vocabulary

1. when[2]
2. to engrave[6]
3. to be going to[7]
4. to remember[10]
5. beach[12]
6. to show[13]
7. asleep[14]
8. dawn[15]
9. blanket[16]
10. sand[19]
11. to look for[20]
12. little tail[26]
13. to share[28]

Translate

1. Yo *tenía / era* ocho años.
2. Me *recuerdo / recordo* aquella noche como si fuera ayer.
3. El cometa va *a / de* pasar hasta dentro de ochenta años.
4. ¿*Por qué / Porque* me estás despertando?
5. Estábamos *sentados / sentandos* en la arena.
6. Él le *puso / pusó* los binoculares.

notes

True or False: 1. F[10] 2. T[12] 3. F[19] 4. F[23] 5. F[27] **Expressions:** ¿por qué? - why? / ¿Qué está pasando? - What's going on? / acaso - maybe / claro - of course / de repente - suddenly / entonces - so / nunca mas - ever again / ya no - not anymore **Multiple Choice:** 1. a[28] 2. b[11-12] 3. c[7] **Vocabulary:** 1. cuando 2. grabar 3. ir a 4. acordarse 5. playa 6. enseñar 7. dormido 8. madrugada 9. cobija 10. arena 11. buscar 12. colita 13. compartir **Translate:** 1. tenía[1] I was eight years old. 2. recuerdo[5] I remember that night as if it were yesterday. 3. a[7] The comet is going to pass by within eighty years. 4. por qué[15] Why are you waking me up? 5. sentados[19] We were sitting on the sand. 6. puso[22] He put gave him the binoculars.

Un Día Cualquiera de Cuando Era Niño

Francisco (Spain)
313 words (146 wpm) — 12

True or False

1. When he was a child, Francisco shared a room with his sister. T ☐ F ☐
2. He liked to get up very early in the morning. T ☐ F ☐
3. His mom took him to school. T ☐ F ☐
4. When he was a child, the streets were very crowded. T ☐ F ☐
5. In his school, classes finished at noon. T ☐ F ☐

Expressions

¡a levantarse!	a little
a eso de	again
a regañadientes	as they were called back then
algo de	at about
apenas	at the latest
como muy tarde	get up!
como se llamaban entonces	gradually
con esfuerzo	hardly
en las afueras	in the suburbs
invierno	on the streets
jugar al balón	play ball
libre de	reluctantly
merendar	to have a snack
otra vez	winter
poco a poco	with great effort
por las calles	without, free from

Multiple Choice

1. Francisco used to have ___ for breakfast.

   a. cookies and milk   c. cookies and tea
   b. cereal and milk   d. cereal and tea

2. In Francisco's school, classes began at ___.

   a. 8:00   c. 9:00
   b. 8:30   d. 9:30

3. Francisco and his friends used to play in ___ after school.

   a. the streets   c. city parks
   b. recreation centers   d. vacant lots

Text

Me gustaría contaros como recuerdo un día cualquiera de cuando era niño.	1	I would like to tell you how I remember a typical day from when I was little.
Vivíamos en Madrid, en una casa humilde en las afueras, al sur de la capital.	2	We lived in Madrid, in a humble house in the suburbs, south of the capital.
Mi hermano y yo dormíamos en la misma habitación.	3	My brother and I slept in the same room.
Todas las mañanas, a eso de las ocho menos cuarto, mi madre entraba en la habitación,	4	Every morning, at about quarter to eight, my mother would enter the room
y nos despertaba: "¡Buenos días!", "¡A levantarse!", "¡Hay que ir a la escuela!"	5	and wake us up, "Good morning!", "Get up!", "You have to go to school!"
Para entonces mi padre ya se había marchado a trabajar.	6	By then, my father had already gone to work.
Hacía algo de frío, especialmente en invierno.	7	It was a little cold, especially in winter.
Con esfuerzo me incorporaba de la cama,	8	With great effort, I would get out of bed,
me vestía sin apenas abrir los ojos,	9	get dressed without hardly opening my eyes,
y me lavaba la cara a regañadientes.	10	and wash my face reluctantly.
En la cocina nos esperaba el desayuno:	11	Breakfast would be waiting for us in the kitchen:
un buen vaso de leche caliente con miel y unas galletas o una magdalena.	12	a nice glass of warm milk with honey and some cookies or a muffin.
A las nueve menos veinte los dos hermanos nos colgábamos nuestras carteras,	13	At 8:40, my brother and I would put on our backpacks,
y juntos marchábamos andando al colegio, los dos solos.	14	and walk to school together, just the two of us.
Éramos pequeños, pero entonces había poco tráfico por las calles.	15	We were small, but then there was little traffic on the streets.
Poco a poco se nos iban juntando los niños de alrededor, que vivían en las calles de camino de la escuela,	16	Gradually, the kids who lived on the streets on the way to school would come join us,
y todos juntos, nos arremolinábamos a la puerta del colegio.	17	and all together, we'd crowd around the school's gate.
Las clases empezaban a las nueve.	18	Classes began at nine.
A las once salíamos al recreo:	19	At eleven, we went to recess:
media hora para jugar con los compañeros y comer algo, normalmente un bocadillo y una fruta.	20	half an hour to play with classmates and eat something, usually a sandwich and a piece of fruit.
Después, dos horas más de clase, otro descanso a mediodía para comer,	21	After that, two hours more of class, another break at noon for lunch,
y otra vez clase de tres a cinco, ésta con un poco más de sueño.	22	and again classes from three to five, this one with a bit more sleep.
Por la tarde merendábamos en casa	23	In the afternoon, we'd have a snack at home,
y si hacía buen tiempo, salíamos a jugar.	24	and if the weather was nice, we'd go out to play.
No era difícil encontrar en el Madrid de aquella época zonas libre de edificios, o descampados, como se llamaban entonces,	25	It wasn't difficult to find, in Madrid in those days, areas without buildings, or "open areas," as they were called back then,

donde jugar al balón, al escondite, o a hacer batallas.	26	to play ball in, or hide-and-seek, or play war.
Después a cenar, y a las diez y media, como muy tarde, ya estábamos acostados, disfrutando de un cuento o de un libro de aventuras.	27	After dinner, at ten-thirty at the latest, we would be in bed already, enjoying a story or an adventure book.

Vocabulary

1. to get out of bed[8] _____
2. cookies[12] _____
3. muffin[12] _____
4. honey[12] _____
5. to join[16] _____
6. to crowd[17] _____
7. recess[19] _____
8. sandwich[20] _____
9. break[21] _____
10. noon[21] _____
11. open areas[25] _____
12. building[25] _____
13. hide-and-seek[26] _____
14. story[27] _____

Translate

1. Todas las mañanas, a las ocho menos cuarto, mi madre *entraba / entró* en la habitación.
2. En la cocina nos esperaba el *desayuno / desayunamiento*.
3. Entonces había poco tráfico *por / a* las calles.
4. A las once *salíamos / salábamos* al recreo.
5. Nos daban media hora *para / por* jugar con los compañeros y comer algo.
6. *Por / En* la tarde merendábamos en casa.

notes

True or False: 1. F[3] 2. F[8] 3. F[14] 4. F[17] 5. F[21] **Expressions:** ¡a levantarse! - get up! / a eso de - at about / a regañadientes - reluctantly / algo de - a little / apenas - hardly / como muy tarde - at the latest / como se llamaban entonces - as they were called back then / con esfuerzo - with great effort / en las afueras - in the suburbs / invierno - winter / jugar al balón - play ball / libre de - without, free from / merendar - to have a snack / otra vez - again / poco a poco - gradually / por las calles - on the streets / **Multiple Choice:** 1. a[12] 2. c[18] 3. d[25] **Vocabulary:** 1. incorporarse de la cama 2. galletas 3. magdalen 4. miel 5. juntarse 6. arremolinarse 7. recreo 8. bocadillo 9. descanso 10. mediodía 11. descampados 12. edificio 13. escondite 14. cuento **Translate:** 1. entraba[4] Every morning, at a quarter to eight, my mother entered the room. 2. desayuno[11] In the kitchen, breakfast was waiting for us. 3. por[15] Then there was little traffic on the streets. 4. salíamos[19] At eleven o'clock, we went out for recess. 5. para[20] They would give us half an hour to play with classmates and eat something. 6. Por[23] In the afternoon, we would have a snack at home.

Vacaciones

Unas Vacaciones en Francia

Jorge (Peru)
418 words (118 wpm) 13

True or False

1. Although Jorge works in tourism, he doesn't travel much. T ☐ F ☐
2. He traveled to see his friends that are studying abroad. T ☐ F ☐
3. His trip to France was a last-minute trip. T ☐ F ☐
4. He had no problems while staying in France. T ☐ F ☐
5. During his trip to Paris, he met a girl that became his girlfriend. T ☐ F ☐

Expressions

¿que más?	as I said before
bajo cero	below zero
casi	fluently
como dije antes	I didn't have much trouble
es la mejor manera	it takes me long
eso es lo que pienso hacer	it's the best way
felizmente	luckily
fluidamente	more than anything
jamás	nearly-quite
más que nada	never
me toma mucho	perhaps
no se me complicó mucho	pretty much
prácticamente	see what it has in store for me
tal vez	since
ver lo que tiene preparado para mí	that's what I intend to do
ya que	what else?

Multiple Choice

1. While in Paris, Jorge didn't see ___.

   a. the Eiffel Tower   c. the Palace of Versailles
   b. the Arc de Triomphe   d. Notre Dame

2. The thing that most interested Jorge during his trip was ___.

   a. the architecture   c. the language
   b. the food   d. the music

3. Now, Jorge is planning his next trip, which will be a longer trip to ___.

   a. the United States   c. China
   b. Europe   d. India

Text

Si tuviera que compartir una experiencia de vacaciones,	1	If I had to share a vacation experience,
para mí sería la última que tuve, que fue mi viaje a Francia.	2	for me, it would be the last one I had, which was my trip to France.
Yo para ser una persona que trabaja en turismo, viajo realmente casi nada.	3	For being a person that works in tourism, I really hardly travel at all.
Eh… he estado al sur del Perú, y al norte del Perú, en cada extremo,	4	Uh… I've been to the south of Peru, and the north of Peru, to each end [of Peru],
pero jamás en mi vida he cruzado la frontera,	5	but I have never in my life crossed the border,
así que mi primer gran viaje fuera del país fue a Francia.	6	so my first big trip outside the country was to France.
El motivo de mi viaje, eh… la mayor motivación, fue el poder ver a mi novia de nuevo,	7	The reason for my trip, uh… my greatest motivation, was being able to see my girlfriend again,
ya que estuvo varios meses viviendo en Perú conmigo.	8	since she spent several months living in Peru with me.
Ella tuvo que regresar a terminar la universidad,	9	She had to return to finish college,
así que yo programé mi viaje casi medio año.	10	so I planned my trip for nearly half a year.
Estaba un poco nervioso realmente porque nunca nunca había salido del país.	11	I was a bit nervous actually because I had never ever been out of the country.
Y especialmente estuve muy preocupado por el tema del idioma.	12	And I was especially very concerned about the language issue.
Eh… yo hablo inglés fluidamente; no tengo problema realmente.	13	Uh… I speak English fluently; I have no problem, really.
Pero jamás en mi vida había hablado francés.	14	But never in my life had I spoken French.
El poco conocimiento que tengo, felizmen… felizmente me ayudó bastante.	15	The little knowledge I have luckil-… luckily helped me a lot.
Em, bueno, también tenía a mi novia a mi lado así que no se me complicó mucho.	16	Well, I also had my girlfriend with me, so I didn't have too much trouble.
Lo que yo pude ver en Francia fue más que nada… em… mi primera parada fue Paris.	17	What I could see in France was more than anything um… my first stop was Paris.
Estuve en Paris una semana; me quedé en la casa de un amigo.	18	I was in Paris for one week; I stayed at a friend's house.
Eh… hice prácticamente todo lo turístico:	19	Uh… I pretty much did all the touristy things.
Vi la torre Eiffel, el Arco del Triunfo.	20	I saw the Eiffel Tower, the Arc de Triomphe,
Eh… Estuve en Notre Dame.	21	Uh… I was at Notre Dame.
Hice Sagrado Corazón, em… ¿que más, que más, que más?	22	I did the Sacred Heart, um… what else, what else, what else?
No pude hacer el Palacio de Versalles.	23	I couldn't do the Palace of Versailles.
Eso es lo que pienso hacer la próxima que vaya.	24	That's what I intend to do the next time I go.
Eh… pero lo que más llamó mi atención fue la comida, como cocinero que soy.	25	Uh… but what caught my attention the most was the food, being the cook I am.

Es la mejor manera de ampliar mi horizonte gastronómico.	26	It's the best way to expand my culinary horizons.	
Tal vez no haya sido la mejor época del año, ya que fue invierno.	27	Perhaps it wasn't the best time of year, as it was winter.	
Uno que está acostumbrado a estar doce grados como más bajo,	28	One who is used to being at 12 degrees [Celsius] at the lowest,	
eh… allá era mucho mucho mucho más terrible en serio.	29	uh… there, it was much, much, much more awful really.	
Estar bajo cero grados es poco agradable.	30	Being below zero degrees is unpleasant.	
Felizmente que no me tomó mucho aclimatarme.	31	Fortunately, it didn't take me long to get acclimated.	
Estuve en total tres meses en Francia.	32	Um… I was in France for a total of three months.	
Vi mucho. Eh… más que nada estuve en el norte.	33	I saw a lot. Uh… more than anything, I was in the north.	
Y, bueno, como dije antes ¿no?, viajé por mi novia,	34	And, well, like I said before, right? I traveled [there] for my girlfriend,	
así que pasé mi… la mayoría de mi tiempo con ella.	35	so I spent my… most of my time with her.	
No hice nada más turístico luego de estar en Paris.	36	I didn't do anything else touristic after being in Paris.	
Eh… aunque ahora estoy programando un viaje de vuelta,	37	Uh… although now I'm planning a trip back,	
esta vez por mucho más tiempo,	38	this time for much longer,	
así que esta vez me gustaría cruzar… cruzar las fronteras,	39	so this I would like to cross… cross some borders,	
y ver qué… qué es lo que Europa tiene preparado para mí.	40	and see what… what Europe has in store for me.	

Vocabulary

1. reason[7] _____
2. to plan[10] _____
3. nervous[11] _____
4. concerned[12] _____
5. with me[16] _____
6. stop[17] _____
7. to stay[18] _____
8. next time[24] _____
9. to catch one's attention[25] _____
10. to expand[26] _____
11. to be used to[28] _____
12. awful[29] _____
13. there[29] _____
14. to get acclimated[31] _____
15. trip back[37] _____
16. to cross[39] _____

Translate

1. Si *tuviera / tendría* que compartir una experiencia de vacaciones sería la última que tuve.
2. Estuvo *varios meses / meses varios* viviendo en Perú *conmigo*.
3. Ella *tuvo / tuve* que regresar a terminar la universidad.
4. Jamás en mi vida había *hablando / hablado* francés.
5. Tal vez no *haya / ha* sido la mejor época del año, ya que fue invierno.
6. Estar bajo cero *grados / grado* es poco agradable.

True or False: 1. T³ 2. F⁷ 3. F¹⁰ 4. T¹⁶ 5. F³⁴ **Expressions:** ¿que más? - what else? / bajo cero - below zero / casi - nearly-quite / como dije antes - as I said before / es la mejor manera - it's the best way / eso es lo que pienso hacer - that's what I intend to do / felizmente - luckily / fluidamente - fluently / jamás - never / más que nada - more than anything / me toma mucho - it takes me long / no se me complicó mucho - I didn't have much trouble / prácticamente - pretty much / tal vez - perhaps / ver lo que tiene preparado para mí - see what it has in store for me / ya que - since **Multiple Choice:** 1. c²³ 2. b²⁵ 3. b⁴⁰
Vocabulary: 1. motivo 2. programar 3. nervioso 4. preocupado 5. a mi lado 6. parada 7. quedarse en 8. la próxima vez 9. llamar su atención 10. ampliar 11. estar acostumbrado 12. terrible 13. allá 14. aclimatarse 15. viaje de vuelta 16. cruzar
Translate: 1. tuviera¹ If I had to share a vacation experience, it would be the last one I had. 2. varios meses⁸ She spent several months living in Peru with me. 3. tuvo⁹ She had to return to finish college. 4. hablando¹⁴ Never in my life had I spoken French. 5. haya²⁷ Maybe it was not the best time of year, as it was winter. 6. grados³⁰ Being below zero degrees is unpleasant.

Trujillo

José (Honduras)
344 words (154 wpm) 🔊 14

True or False

1. José is talking about a trip that he and his wife made when she was pregnant with their first child. T ☐ F ☐
2. He is talking about a camping holiday. T ☐ F ☐
3. It rained for all three days during their stay in Trujillo. T ☐ F ☐
4. The first day, José and his family were forced to stay indoors because there was a rainstorm. T ☐ F ☐
5. He went to Trujillo to enjoy the sea and the sun. T ☐ F ☐

Expressions

a (seis) horas de	(six) hours from
a mediodía	a little
al regreso	a little tired
algo cansado	approximately
anteriormente	at noon
aproximadamente	at that time
aun mejor	earlier
bastante	even better
bastante fuerte	I like traveling
de pronto	not anymore
de regreso	on the way back
el día en que nos veníamos	once we got home
en aquel momento	pretty hard
eso es lo a que fuimos	quite
lamentablemente	suddenly
me gusta irme de viaje	the day we were coming back home
un poco	this is what we went for
ya no	unfortunately

Multiple Choice

1. They went to Trujillo during ___.
   a. St. Joseph's week
   b. the Christmas holidays
   c. the Easter holidays
   d. *none of the above*

2. On the way back, they ate ___.
   a. roast chicken   b. grilled meat   c. boiled meat   d. smoked ribs

3. When they got home from the trip, José felt ___.
   a. stressed out   b. relaxed   c. sick   d. tired

Text

Unas vacaciones que recuerdo bastante fue una vez que fuimos con mi familia a la ciudad de Trujillo, aquí en Honduras.	1	A vacation that I remember well was one time when my family and I went to the city of Trujillo, here in Honduras.
Trujillo queda aproximadamente a seis horas de donde vivo,	2	Trujillo is approximately six hours from where I live,
lo cual me emociona mucho porque como les dije anteriormente, me gusta mucho viajar.	3	which excites me because, as I said earlier, I love traveling.
Me gusta mucho agarrar mi vehículo e irme de viaje.	4	I love to take my car and go traveling.
En aquel momento solamente teníamos a nuestro hijo mayor.	5	At that time, we only had our eldest son.
Era en la Semana Santa de ese año.	6	It was at Easter of that year.
Pues nos fuimos en el camino.	7	So, we took to the road.
Nos hospedamos… hicimos las reservaciones de hotel.	8	We stayed… we made hotel reservations.
Nos quedamos en el hotel.	9	We stayed at the hotel.
Lamentablemente, la primera… el primer día que llegamos, estaba lloviendo bastante fuerte.	10	Unfortunately, the first… the first day we arrived, it was raining pretty hard.
Por lo tanto el mar estaba bien picado—estaba sucio.	11	So, the sea was very choppy—it was dirty.
No se podía, de hecho, nadar en el mar.	12	We couldn't really swim in the sea.
Mi hijo estaba muy emocionado.	13	My son was really excited.
Él quería meterse al agua.	14	He wanted to get into the water.
Pero, tengo fotografías de él en la playa pero con suéter, con ropa de frío,	15	But, I have pictures of him on the beach but with a sweater, cool-weather clothes,
porque estaba haciendo frío; estaba lloviendo.	16	because it was getting cold; it was raining.
Eso fue el primer día.	17	That was the first day.
Pero bueno, igual disfrutamos ir a la ciudad.	18	But, well, we also enjoyed going to the city.
Trujillo es una ciudad muy linda. Es una ciudad colonial.	19	Trujillo is a very beautiful city. It is a colonial city.
Fuimos, compramos algunos souvenirs, y fue bastante, bastante bonito.	20	We went and bought some souvenirs, and it was really quite beautiful.
Ya el segundo día no llovió tanto.	21	The second day, it didn't rain as much.
Estaba siempre nublado, eso sí, pero ya no llovía tanto.	22	It was overcast, yes, but it wasn't raining so much anymore.
Ya para el tercer día, que era el día en que nos veníamos, hizo un sol bellísimo.	23	And the third day, which was the day we were coming [back home], it was sunny and beautiful.
Pudimos meternos al mar.	24	We were able to go to the sea.
El día anterior nos metimos al mar, pero el mar estaba… todavía estaba un poco sucio.	25	The day before we went to the sea, but the sea was… it was still a little dirty.
No estaba haciendo sol.	26	It wasn't sunny.
De pronto empezó a llover un poco.	27	Suddenly it started to rain a little.

Ya el día siguiente, que era el día que nos veníamos, a mediodía, antes de eso decidimos meternos en el mar,	28	And the next day, the day we were coming back, at noon, before [coming back], we decided to go into the sea,	
porque a eso…a eso es que fuimos.	29	because that… that is what we went for.	
Y pues nadamos, la pasamos muy bien.	30	And then we swam and had a good time.	
Fue unas vacaciones muy lindas.	31	It was a very nice vacation.	
Al regreso pasamos por otra ciudad que se llama Tocoa, donde nos comimos un delicioso… una deliciosa carne asada.	32	On the way back, we passed another city called Tocoa, where we ate delicious… delicious grilled meat.	
Estuvo muy bueno.	33	It was very good.	
Y ya de regreso pues veníamos algo cansados.	34	And when we got home, we were a little tired.	
Mi hijo estaba emocionado.	35	My son was excited.	
Le gustó mucho el viaje.	36	He really enjoyed the trip.	
Y fue unas vacaciones que… la verdad que siempre voy a recordar,	37	And it was a vacation that… really, I will always remember,	
y espero tener vacaciones aún mejores.	38	and I hope to have even better vacations [in the future].	

Vocabulary

1. which[3] _____
2. eldest son[5] _____
3. to take the road[7] _____
4. to stay[8] _____
5. to rain[10] _____
6. choppy sea[11] _____
7. dirty[11] _____
8. excited[13] _____
9. to get into the water[14] _____
10. sweater[15] _____
11. overcast[22] _____
12. somewhat, a little[34] _____

Translate

1. Eso me emociona mucho porque como les *dije / he dijo* anteriormente, me gusta mucho viajar.
2. El mar *estaba / estuviera* bien picado.
3. No se podía, *de / en* hecho, nadar en el mar.
4. Él quería meterse *en el / al agua*.
5. Estaba siempre nublado, pero ya no *llovía / lluviaba* tanto.
6. Antes de eso decidimos *meternos / nos meter* en el mar.

True or False: 1. F[5] 2. F[9] 3. F[10] 4. F[18] 5. T[29] **Expressions:** a (seis) horas de - (six) hours from / a mediodía - at noon / al regreso - on the way back / algo cansados - we were a little tired / anteriormente - earlier / aproximadamente - approximately aun mejor - even better / bastante - quite / bastante fuerte - pretty hard / de pronto - suddenly / de regreso - once we got home / el día en que nos veníamos - the day we were coming back home / en aquel momento - at that time / eso es lo a que fuimos - this is what we went for / lamentablemente - unfortunately / me gusta irme de viaje - I like traveling / un poco - a little / ya no - not anymore **Multiple Choice:** 1. c[6] 2. b[32] 3. d[34] **Vocabulary:** 1. lo cual 2. hijo mayor 3. irse en el camino 4. hospedarse 5. llover 6. mar picado 7. sucio 8. emocionado 9. meterse al agua 10. suéter 11. nublado 12. algo **Translate:** 1. dije[3] That excites me a lot because as I told you before, I really like to travel. 2. estaba[11] The sea was very choppy. 3. de[12] You could not, in fact, swim in the sea. 4. en el[14] He wanted to get into the water. 5. llovía[22] It was still cloudy, but it wasn't raining so much anymore. 6. meternos[28] Before that, we decided to go into the sea.

notes

Buzios

Florencia (Argentina)
340 words (142 wpm) 🔊 15

True or False

1. In Buzios, people often eat on the beach. T☐ F☐
2. In Buzios, the weather is quite terrible in the winter. T☐ F☐
3. When Florencia and her husband went to Buzios, the weather was very hot. T☐ F☐
4. It rains a lot in Buzios. T☐ F☐
5. She finds the sound of the sea waves irritating. T☐ F☐

Expressions

a fines de marzo	actually
con alguna frecuencia	actually, the truth is that...
demasiado	because
en realidad	but still
hablar de	in late March
la verdad que	personally
lo que más me gusta es	quite often
particularmente	so many
pero aún así	supposedly
porque	to talk about
supuestamente	too (much)
tantos	what I like most is...
todo el año	year-round

Multiple Choice

1. Florencia went to Brazil to celebrate her ___.

    a. sweet sixteen   c. birthday
    b. graduation   d. honeymoon

2. The northern part of the city is ___ than the southern one.

    a. quieter   c. safer
    b. more interesting   d. more dangerous

3. Which of the following is true about Buzios?

    a. The locals are not particularly friendly toward tourists.
    b. The weather is very changeable.
    c. Peddlers are not allowed on its beaches.
    d. *all of the above*

Text

1	¡Hola! Mi nombre es Florencia, y soy de Buenos Aires, Argentina.	Hello, my name is Florencia, and I'm from Buenos Aires, Argentina.
2	Eh... voy a hablar un poco de mis vacaciones.	Uh... I'm going to talk a little about my vacation.
3	Las vacaciones favoritas que pasé, en realidad, eh... fue mi luna de miel.	My favorite vacation I've taken, actually, uh... was my honeymoon.
4	Eh... con mi esposo nos fuimos a... a Buzios, Brasil.	Uh... my husband and I went to... to Buzios, Brazil.
5	Y Buzios es un lugar donde está cerca de la playa.	And Buzios is a place close to the beach.
6	Y hay una parte norte y una parte sur—	And there is a northern part and a southern part—
7	una parte en el norte de playas y del sur, que se diferencian,	a northern beach and a southern one, which differ,
8	porque en la parte norte es más tranquilo— no hay tantas olas—y en el sur hay más olas.	because in the northern part it is quieter— there are not many waves—and in the south, there are more waves.
9	Básicamente, todo lo que hay para hacer es estar en el mar.	Basically, all there is to do is be at the seaside.
10	Eh... hay vendedores ambulantes que te traen distintos tipos de comida.	Uh... there are peddlers that bring you different types of food.
11	Hay muchas frutas exóticas y diferentes.	There are many exotic and different fruits.
12	Eh... es un clima ideal todo... todo el año.	Uh... it is an ideal climate all... year-round.
13	Nosotros fuimos en... a fines de marzo,	We went in... in late March,
14	y supuestamente era un... un clima cálido pero no... no demasiado caluroso,	and it supposedly had... warm weather but not... not too hot,
15	pero aún así te permitía a estar en el mar.	but still allowed you to be by the sea.
16	Y lo único que sucede en estos lugares es que suele llover eh... con alguna frecuencia,	And all that happens in these places is that it usually rains uh... quite often,
17	o durante el día hay distintos tipos de clima.	or during the day there are different types of weather.
18	Pero, la verdad que me encantó Brasil por su hospitalidad,	But really I loved Brazil for their hospitality,
19	por la... lo alegres que son y los buenos anfitriones,	for... how happy they are and such good hosts,
20	cómo te tratan como turista.	how they treat you as a tourist.
21	La verdad que... que es muy lindo Brasil.	Brazil is really very lovely.
22	Son muy alegres, son muy festivos.	They are very cheerful, very festive.
23	Em... la pasamos muy, muy bien.	Um... we had a very, very good time.
24	En realidad lo que más me gusta es poder estar en la playa, el ruido del mar.	Actually, what I like the most is being able to be on the beach, the sound of the sea.
25	Las olas son tan tranquilizadoras y te desconectan.	The waves are so soothing and disconnecting.
26*	Y podés estar en otro... otro ambiente y poder parar.	And you can be in a different place and get some rest

	Yo creo que las vacaciones deberían ser más que un deseo: un derecho.	27	I believe that vacations should be more than a want: [they should be] a right.
	Todos deberíamos tomarnos vacaciones porque es saludable,	28	We should all take vacations because it is healthy;
	porque es bueno desconectarse y romper con las rutinas y poder hacer lo que a uno más le gusta, ¿no?	29	it is good to disconnect and take a break from routines and to be able to do what you like most, right?
	Y bueno, a mí particularmente en la playa, los días cálidos, los días de calor, poder estar en... frente al mar y escuchar las olas es lo que más me relaja y más me desconecta.	30	Well, to me personally, be on the beach, warm days, hot days, being able to be on the oceanfront, listening to the waves, is what relaxes me most and helps me disconnect the most.

*26 podés is the voseo conjugation. (See 'voseo' on Wikipedia for more information.)

Vocabulary

1. honeymoon[3] _____
2. wave[8] _____
3. mobile, walking[10] _____
4. warm[14] _____
5. hot[14] _____
6. allow to[15] _____
7. to tend to[16] _____
8. host[19] _____
9. to have a good time[23] _____
10. sound, noise[24] _____
11. calming[25] _____
12. right[27] _____
13. wish, want[27] _____
14. healthy[28] _____

Translate

1. Voy a hablar *de / en* mis vacaciones.
2. Con mi esposo nos *fuimos / fueramos* a Buzios.
3. Las playas se *diferencian / diferenten*.
4. El clima es cálido pero no demasiado *caluroso / calurosa*.
5. El clima te permitía *a / -* estar en el mar.
6. La pasamos muy *bien / buenos*.

notes

True or False: 1. T[10] 2. F[12] 3. F[14] 4. T[16] 5. F[24] **Expressions:** a fines de marzo - in late March / con alguna frecuencia - quite often / demasiado - too (much) / en realidad - actually / hablar de - to talk about / la verdad que - actually, the truth is that... / lo que más me gusta es - what I like most is... / particularmente - personally / pero aún así - but still / porque - because / supuestamente - supposedly / tantos - so many / todo el año - year-round **Multiple Choice:** 1. d[3] 2. a[8] 3. b[17] **Vocabulary:** 1. luna de miel 2. ola 3. ambulante 4. cálido 5. caluroso 6. permeter 7. soler 8. anfitrión 9. pasarla bien 10. ruido 11. tranquilizador 12. derecho 13. deseo 14. saludable **Translate:** 1. de[2] I'm going to talk about my vacation. 2. fuimos[4] My husband and I went to Buzios. 3. diferencian[7] The beaches differ. 4. caluroso[14] The climate is warm but not too hot. 5. a[15] The climate allowed you to be at sea. 6. bien[23] We had a great time.

Mi Ciudad

La Ciudad de México

Sandra (Mexico)
406 words (126 wpm)   🔘 16

True or False

1. One of the major problems of Mexico City is the widespread crime. T☐ F☐
2. Mexico City has a subway system. T☐ F☐
3. Metrobus is the best means of transportation in Mexico City because it reaches any corner of the city. T☐ F☐
4. In Mexico City, people hardly ever get bored. T☐ F☐
5. Sandra says that the food in Mexico City isn't particularly good. T☐ F☐

Expressions

al parecer	apparently
debes de	are packed
dejar tu auto abierto	causes many problems
en cuanto a	in the last few years
en los últimos años	it is considered
en quince minutos	regarding
es considerado	that's why
es por esto que	there won't be any problem.
están muy llenos	to be careful
no habrá ningún problema	to leave your car unlocked
ocasiona bastantes problemas	within 15 minutes
puedes conseguir	you can get
tener precaución	you must

Multiple Choice

1. Mexico City is the ___ most populated city in the world.
   - a. second
   - b. third
   - c. fourth
   - d. tenth

2. In Mexico City, many people still use their car because ___.
   - a. public transportation is expensive
   - b. gasoline is cheap
   - c. public transportation is overcrowded
   - d. the government incentivizes car ownership

3. Which of the following is true about Mexico City?
   - a. The traffic is a big problem.
   - b. There are many museums
   - c. There are many free activities.
   - d. *all of the above*

Text

Les voy a hablar un poco de la ciudad donde yo nací y crecí.	1	I am going to talk a little about the city where I was born and grew up.
Yo eh... soy de la Ciudad de México, que es considerada al parecer la tercera ciudad más poblada del mundo.	2	I uh... am from Mexico City, which is considered, I think, the third most populated city in the world.
Tiene alrededor de veinte millones de habitantes, lo cual ocasiona bastantes problemas.	3	It has about 20 million inhabitants, which causes many problems.
Uno de los problemas más grandes de la ciudad es el tráfico.	4	One of the city's biggest problems is its traffic;
En la Ciudad de México hay muchas opciones para transportarse.	5	In Mexico City, there are many options to get around.
Tenemos el... los autobuses, taxis, el metro; tenemos el metrobús que es un camión que tiene su propia carril... su propio carril en las calles.	6	We have the... the buses, taxis, the subway; we have the "metrobus," which is a bus that has its own lane... its own lane on the streets.
Entonces es un medio de transporte rápido pero no... no hay líneas en toda la ciudad,	7	So, it is a fast means of transportation, but there... there aren't routes everywhere in the city,
y además eh... siempre está muy lleno.	8	and also uh... it's always crowded.
El metro, el metrobús, los autobuses siempre son... están muy llenos.	9	The subway, the Metrobús, the buses are always... are packed.
Es por esto que mucha gente prefiere utilizar su automóvil,	10	That's why many people prefer to use their car.
pero es otro problema porque siempre encuentras mucho tráfico.	11	But that's another issue because you always find a lot of traffic.
Un trayecto que sin tráfico tú podrías llegar a algún lugar en quince minutos, con el tráfico se puede hacer de hasta dos horas.	12	A journey which without traffic you could make it somewhere within 15 minutes, with traffic it can take you up to two hours.
Entonces el tráfico es una de las grandes desventajas de la Ciudad de México.	13	So, traffic is one of the big disadvantages of Mexico City.
Em... algunas de las ventajas que tiene vivir en una ciudad tan grande como la Ciudad de México es que hay muchas cosas que hacer.	14	Um... some of the advantages that living in a city as big as Mexico City has is that there are many things to do.
Hay muchos museos, muchas tiendas, muchas actividades.	15	There are many museums, many shops, many activities.
De hecho eh... el gobierno de la Ciudad de México ofrece muchas actividades que puedes hacer gratuitas con tu familia.	16	In fact uh... the government of Mexico City offers many activities that you can do for free with your family.
Y eh... el centro de la Ciudad de México en los últimos años se ha vuelto un lugar que atrae a muchos jóvenes,	17	And uh... downtown Mexico City in the last few years has become a place that attracts a lot of young people
porque hay... han estado abriendo muchos antros y muchos bares nuevos.	18	because there are... they have been opening many clubs and new bars.
Entonces los jóvenes los fines de semana por las noches... es un centro de reunión para muchos jóvenes.	19	So, young people at night on the weekends... it's a get-together spot for many young people.

En cuanto a la seguridad en la Ciudad de México, en los últimos años se ha vuelto un poco más peligroso,	20	Regarding security in Mexico City, in recent years, it has become a little more dangerous,
pero es como todas las grandes ciudades.	21	but it's like in all major cities.
Debes de tener precaución en algunas colonias que son más peligrosas,	22	You have to be careful in some areas that are more dangerous.
Y lo que debes de hacer en cualquier lugar, ¿no?:	23	And what you have to do anywhere, right?, [is]:
Ser... ser precavido; no dejar tu auto abierto; no ir por la noche en lugares solos.	24	Be... be careful; don't leave your car unlocked; don't wander around isolated places at night.
Entonces, si tienes este tipo de precauciones no... no habrá ningún problema.	25	So, if you take this kind of precautions there... there won't be any problem.
Lo que más me gusta de la Ciudad de México es... su comida y que encuentras comida fresca en cualquier lugar.	26	What I like the most about Mexico City is... its food and that you [can] find fresh food anywhere.
Hay muchos mercados donde puedes conseguir comida fresca, y la comida en la Ciudad de México es muy rica.	27	There are many markets where you can get fresh food, and the food in Mexico City is very good.

Vocabulary

1. to get around[5] _____
2. lane[6] _____
3. fast[7] _____
4. crowded, full[8] _____
5. journey[12] _____
6. disadvantage[13] _____
7. advantage[14] _____
8. for free[16] _____
9. club[18] _____
10. get-together spot[19] _____
11. area, neighborhood[22] _____
12. forewarned[24] _____
13. precautions[25] _____
14. fresh food[27] _____

Translate

1. Les voy a hablar un poco de la ciudad donde yo - / *me* nací.
2. Los autobuses siempre *están / son* muy llenos.
3. Un trayecto que sin tráfico tú *podrías / pudieras* llegar a algún lugar en quince minutos, con el tráfico se puede hacer de hasta dos horas.
4. El gobierno de la Ciudad de México ofrece muchas actividades que puedes hacer *gratuitas / por gratuito* con tu familia.
5. En los ultimos años han estado *abriendo / abierto* muchos antros y muchos bares nuevos.
6. Debes *de / que* tener precaución en algunas colonias que son más peligrosas.

notes

True or False: 1. F⁴ 2. T⁶ 3. F⁷ 4. T¹⁴ 5. F²⁷ **Expressions:** al parecer - apparently / debes de - you must / dejar tu auto abierto - to leave your car unlocked / en cuanto a - regarding / en los últimos años - in the last few years / en quince minutos - within 15 minutes / es considerado - it is considered / es por esto que - that's why / están muy llenos - are packed / no habrá ningún problema - there won't be any problem. / ocasiona bastantes problemas - causes many problems / puedes conseguir - you can get / tener precaución - to be careful **Multiple Choice:** 1. b² 2. c⁹⁻¹⁰ 3. d¹³,¹⁵⁻¹⁶ **Vocabulary:** 1. transportarse 2. carril 3. rápido 4. lleno 5. trayecto 6. desventaja 7. ventaja 8. gratuito 9. antro 10. centro de reunión 11. colonia 12. precavido 13. precauciones 14. comida fresca **Translate:** 1. -¹ I'm going to talk a bit about the city where I was born. 2. están⁹ The buses are always very full. 3. podrías¹² A journey that, without traffic, you could get someplace in fifteen minutes, with traffic can take up to two hours. 4. gratuitas¹⁶ The government of Mexico City offers many activities that you can do for free with your family. 5. abriendo¹⁸ In recent years, they have been opening lots of clubs and new bars. 6. de²² You must have caution in some areas that are more dangerous.

Madrid

Francisco (Spain)
367 words (145 wpm)
🔘 17

True or False

1. In Madrid, the weather is always warm, so it never snows there.   T ☐ F ☐
2. Madrid is especially busy with tourists in the fall.   T ☐ F ☐
3. Madrid is the most important Spanish city.   T ☐ F ☐
4. The urban area is the most visited part of the city.   T ☐ F ☐
5. Madrid hosts some of the most important museums in the world.   T ☐ F ☐

Expressions

además de	a number of
entre otros	among others
está lleno de	in addition to, not to mention
formado por	it is full of
justo en el centro	it is located
miles de	made up of
se encuentra	recently
últimamente	right in the middle
una serie de	thousands of

Multiple Choice

1. Which of the following is true about Madrid?

    a. It's very cosmopolitan.
    b. Its population is over six million.
    c. It's very quiet for a big city.
    d. It's the second largest city in Spain.

2. Francisco mentions that he ___ in Madrid.

    a. was born
    b. went to university
    c. got married
    d. *all of the above*

3. Which of the following is not a major attraction in Madrid?

    a. Paseo del Prado
    b. The Prado Museum
    c. The Picasso Museum
    d. Puerta del Sol

Text

Nací en Madrid, la capital de España.	1	I was born in Madrid, the capital of Spain.
Madrid es una gran ciudad, con más de tres millones de habitantes.	2	Madrid is a big city, with more than three million inhabitants.
Se encuentra al sur de la sierra de Guadarrama, en cuyas cumbres vemos nieve en el invierno,	3	It is located south of the Guadarrama Mountains, whose peaks we see snow on in the winter,
y al norte del río Tajo, donde empieza la meseta sur y La Mancha, la tierra de Don Quijote.	4	and north of the river Tagus, where the southern plateau and La Mancha, the land of Don Quixote, begin.
Madrid es una ciudad amable y bulliciosa,	5	Madrid is a friendly, bustling city,

formada por habitantes que fueron llegando de toda España—casi no hay madrileños de dos generaciones—	6	made up of people coming from all over Spain—there are almost no second-generation Madrilenians—
y en los últimos años, de todo el mundo, principalmente de Hispanoamérica, el norte y centro de África y de Europa del Este;	7	and in recent years, from all over the world, mainly from Latin America, northern and central Africa, and eastern Europe;
también hay muchos chinos últimamente.	8	there have also been many Chinese recently.
Eso la ha convertido en una ciudad abierta y cosmopolita donde nadie se siente extraño y todo el mundo convive bastante bien.	9	This has made it an open, cosmopolitan city where nobody feels foreign, and everyone coexists pretty well.
Madrid está llena de opciones de entretenimiento: cines, teatros, salas de conciertos.	10	Madrid is full of entertainment options: cinemas, theaters, concert halls.
Todos los días es posible realizar alguna actividad de ocio.	11	Every day you can pursue some leisure activity.
Cada verano, miles de turistas se desplazan a la capital para disfrutar de todo su esplendor,	12	Every summer, thousands of tourists travel to the capital to enjoy its splendor,
pasando las horas de más calor entre bares y rincones típicos y disfrutando de su arquitectura, sus museos y su vida nocturna.	13	spending the hottest hours between bars and popular spots and enjoying its architecture, museums, and nightlife.
Económicamente, es la ciudad más importante de España.	14	Economically, it is the most important city in Spain.
Millones de personas acuden a trabajar aquí diariamente.	15	Millions of people come to work here every day.
¡Madrid nunca se detiene!	16	Madrid never stops!
Es una ciudad muy bien comunicada:	17	It has great transport.
Tiene un gran aeropuerto, unas líneas de cercanías que cubren toda la provincia,	18	It has a large airport, commuter lines covering the whole province,
y una carreteras que le comunican con el resto de España y con Europa.	19	and roads that connect it with the rest of Spain and Europe.
El centro histórico de Madrid es el que más visitas recibe, entre otras por su famoso Paseo del Prado.	20	The historic center of Madrid is what received the most visits, among other things, for its famous Paseo del Prado.
En el Paseo del Prado se aglutinan una serie de museos importantísimos a nivel internacional.	21	In the Paseo del Prado there are, grouped together, a number of museums that are significant at an international level.
El Museo del Prado, que compite con el Museo del Louvre, o con el Metropolitan, o con los más importantes del mundo,	22	The Prado Museum, which rivals the Louvre or the Metropolitan, or the most important [museums] in the world,
y luego están el Museo de Arte Moderno Reina Sofía y el Museo Thyssen-Bornemisza, además de muchos centros culturales.	23	and then there are the Museum of Modern Art Reina Sofia and the Thyssen-Bornemisza Museum, and many cultural centers.
Y el gran polo de atracción de Madrid es la Puerta del Sol.	24	And the big center of attraction in Madrid is the Puerta del Sol.
Es el centro de Madrid: la plaza que está justo en el centro de Madrid y justo en el centro de España, el centro de la Península Ibérica.	25	It is the center of Madrid: the square right in the middle of Madrid, right in the middle of Spain, the middle of the Iberian Peninsula.

Otro día os cuento más cosas de Madrid. ¡Hasta luego!

26

Another day I'll tell you more about Madrid. Bye!

Vocabulary

1. peak[3] _____
2. whose[3] _____
3. river[4] _____
4. bustling[5] _____
5. foreigner, stranger[9] _____
6. to become[9] _____
7. leisure activity[11] _____
8. to travel to[12] _____
9. to resort to[15] _____
10. to stop[16] _____
11. commuter lines[18] _____
12. to be grouped[21] _____

Translate

1. Yo - / me nací en Madrid, la capital de España.
2. Madrid es una ciudad formada por / de habitantes que fueron llegando de toda España.
3. Últimamente también hay muchos chinos / chineses.
4. Eso la ha convertido en / a una ciudad abierta y cosmopolita.
5. Miles de turistas se desplazan a la capital para / - disfrutar de todo su esplendor.
6. El Museo del Prado, - / se compite con el Museo del Louvre.

notes

True or False: 1. F[3] 2. F[12] 3. T[14] 4. F[20] 5. T[21] **Expressions:** además de - in addition to, not to mention / entre otros - among others / está lleno de - it is full of / formado por - made up of / justo en el centro - right in the middle / miles de - thousands of / se encuentra - it is located / últimamente - recently / una serie de - a number of **Multiple Choice:** 1. a[7] 2. a[1] 3. c[20-24] **Vocabulary:** 1. cumbre 2. cuyo 3. río 4. bullicioso 5. extraño 6. convertirse en 7. actividad de ocio 8. desplazarse a 9. acudira 10. detenerse 11. líneas de cercanías 12. aglutinarse **Translate:** 1. -[1] I was born in Madrid, the capital of Spain. 2. por[6] Madrid is a city made up of inhabitants coming from all over Spain. 3. chinos[8] Lately, there are also many Chinese. 4. en[9] That has made it an open and cosmopolitan city. 5. para[12] Thousands of tourists travel to the capital to enjoy all of its splendor. 6. -[22] The Prado Museum rivals the Louvre Museum.

Buenos Aires

Florencia (Argentina)
551 words (142 wpm) 🔘 18

True or False

1. Florencia says that Los Angeles reminds her of Buenos Aires. T ☐ F ☐
2. Most Latin Americans dislikes spicy food. T ☐ F ☐
3. In Buenos Aires, restaurants usually close at 9 p.m. T ☐ F ☐
4. Buenos Aires is a very clean city. T ☐ F ☐
5. If you go to Buenos Aires, it will be easy to make new friends. T ☐ F ☐

Expressions

¡Qué más pudo pedir!	What else could you ask for!
a esa hora	at that time
a veces	at times
así que	so, therefore
bastante	quite, fairly
cerca de	near
colectivo	bus
creo que	I think that...
en cualquier lado/lugar	anywhere
en ese sentido	in that sense
en general	in general
la mayoría de	most
la verdad que	actually, the truth is that...
picante	spicy
por (2x)	by / because of
propio de	typical of
recién	just, only
sin ningún problema	without any problem

Multiple Choice

1. According to Florencia, Argentinian people are similar to ___.
    a. Italians   b. Germans   c. Californians   d. the French

2. Florencia mentions that you can sense the European influence in the ___ of Buenos Aires.
    a. food   b. architecture   c. people   d. *all of the above*

3. What does Florencia mention about Buenos Aires?
    a. Its population is nearly six million.
    b. Its residents are reserved and introverted.
    c. Businesses close early for siesta.
    d. *none of the above*

Text

¡Hola! Mi nombre es Florencia.	1	Hello! My name is Florencia.
Soy de Buenos Aires, Argentina.	2	I'm from Buenos Aires, Argentina.

Voy a hablar un poco de mi ciudad.	3	I'm going to talk a little about my city.
La verdad que Buenos Aires es una ciudad, eh... creo que de las ciudades de Latinoamérica, es la más parecida a Europa,	4	The truth is that Buenos Aires is a city... uh, I think from among the cities of Latin America, is the one most like Europe,
por la gran inmigración que tuvo de españoles e italianos básicamente,	5	because of the great immigration of Spaniards and Italians basically,
algunos franceses, algunos, este... alemanes, pero básicamente italianos y españoles.	6	some French, some, um... Germans, but mainly Italians and Spaniards.
Así que es una ciudad en que esa influencia se ve reflejado en la comida, en la arquitectura, en la manera de ser.	7	So, it's a city where this influence is reflected in the food, the architecture, the way we are.
Eh... por ejemplo, comemos mucha pasta;	8	Uh, for example, we eat a lot of pasta;
eh... nos expresamos y hablamos con las manos,	9	uh, we express ourselves speaking with our hands,
somos muy de gesticular, muy italianos en ese sentido;	10	very gesticulative, very Italian in that sense;
no comemos picante como la mayoría de los latinoamericanos come.	11	we do not eat spicy [food] as most of Latin American does.
Y em... otra cosa más, es la arquitectura, ¿no?	12	And um... another thing is the architecture, right?
Hay mucha influencia europea en distintos eh... lugares.	13	There is a lot of European influence in different uh... places.
Em... hay ciudades... por ejemplo, la ciudad de La Plata, que es una ciudad cerca de Buenos Aires,	14	Um... there are towns... for example, the city of La Plata, a town near Buenos Aires,
ha sido estudiada y planeada por un francés, un arquitecto francés.	15	has been studied and planned by a Frenchman, a French architect.
Así que tiene toda esa influencia y toda esa caracterización propia de la arquitectura francesa.	16	So, it has all that influence and all that characterization typical of French architecture.
Es una ciudad que está despierta todo el día, digamos.	17	It is a city that is awake the entire day, I'd say.
Eh... cenamos tarde, cenamos a las nueve de la noche, diez de la noche,	18	Uh... we have dinner later, at nine or ten p.m.,
así que recién los restaurantes empiezan a llenarse a esa hora.	19	so restaurants just start to fill up at that time.
Uno puede salir a la una, a las dos de la mañana y... y estar en una avenida con gente.	20	You can go out at one or two in the morning and... and be in a street full of people,
Eh... luces, tiene muchas luces; hay muchas atracciones; hay una avenida llena de teatros.	21	Uh... lights, it has many lights; there are many attractions; there is a street full of theaters.
Podríamos decir que en términos de ciudad se parece mucho New York.	22*	We could say that, in terms of a city, New York is very similar.
pero más... un poco más chica que New York y un poco más sucia también que New York.	23	But more... a little smaller than New York and a little dirtier, too.
Pero, es una ciudad llena de... de gente que es muy amigable,	24	But it is a city full of... of people who are very friendly,

que es muy buena con los turistas, que en general siempre se lleva bien o trata de hacerse entender.	25	who are very good with tourists, who generally always get along or try to make themselves understood.
Eh... uno puede hacerse amigos en cualquier lugar:	26	Uh... one can make friends anywhere:
en la parada de colectivos, en... en un almacén, en cualquier lado uno puede empezar una conversación,	27	at the bus stop, at... at a store, anywhere you can start a conversation,
del clima, de... de la política, de la economía, de lo que pase.	28	about weather, politics, economy, on whatever is going on.
Y sin ningún problema uno puede entable-... -cer... establecer una conversación con alguien em.. fácilmente como... como si nada.	29	Without any problem, you can str-... start a conversation, um... easily as... as if it were nothing.
Em... la ciudad en general está eh... está poblada de gente que es... que está apurada, que trabaja en la oficina en el centro, en el microcentro, lo que se llama microcentro.	30	Um... the city, in general, is uh... it is full of people who are... who are in a hurry, who work in offices downtown, in the micro center, what is called "microcentro."
Y... y después, a eso de las seis de la tarde, el tránsito es un caos.	31	And... and then, at six o'clock in the afternoon, traffic is a mess.
Hay muchos medios de transporte, como trenes, subtes y colectivos, eh... que son los micros o los ómnibus y...	32	There are many ways of public transportation, such as trains, subways, and buses, uh... that is, the minibusses or buses and...
Pero a esa hora, todo es un caos, como que todo se colapsa.	33	But at that time, everything is a mess, like, everything collapses.
Así que hay muchos habitantes—la Argentina tiene cuarenta millones de habitantes—	34	So, there are a lot of people—Argentina has 40 million inhabitants—
y por lo menos once o doce viven en la Capital Federal y en el conurbano, o sea en los alrededores.	35*	and at least 11 to 12 living in the Federal Capital and in the suburbs or nearby.
Así que es una ciudad bastante grande.	36	So, it's a fairly large city.
Y... y es un país bastante concentrado en la ciudad, cerca del puerto.	37	And... and it's a country fairly concentrated in the city, near the port.
Y... bueno, es una ciudad que tiene sus encantos.	38	And... well, it's a city that has its charms.
Eh... la gente es muy efusiva, muy expresiva y... muy loca, a veces.	39	Uh... the people are very effusive, very expressive, and... at times, very crazy.
Hay gen-... hay distintos tipos de personas.	40	There are peop-... there are different types of people.
Pero, la verdad es que me encanta Buenos Aires.	41	But the truth is that I love Buenos Aires.
Es una ciudad de... de tango, de buena carne y ¡qué más pudo pedir!	42	It's a city of good tango and meat. What else could you ask for!

*22 New York would more commonly be called Nueva York in Spanish.

*35 la Capital Federal = Buenos Aires

Vocabulary

1. similar to[4] _____
2. spicy[11] _____
3. awake[17] _____
4. awake[18] _____
5. avenue[20] _____
6. full of[21] _____
7. small[23] _____
8. dirty[23] _____
9. friendly[24] _____
10. to get along[25] _____
11. to try to[25] _____
12. warehouse[27] _____
13. weather[28] _____
14. to be in a hurry[30] _____
15. traffic[31] _____
16. subway[32] _____
17. suburbs[35] _____

Translate

1. Buenos Aires es la ciudad más parecida *a / en* Europa.
2. La plata es una ciudad cerca *de / a* Buenos Aires.
3. La ciudad está *despierta / despertada* todo el día.
4. Buenos Aires es más chica *que / de* New York.
5. La ciudad está poblada *de / con* gente apurada.
6. Hay *distintos tipos / tipos distintos* de personas.

notes

True or False: 1. F[22] 2. F[11] 3. F[19] 4. F[23] 5. T[26] **Expressions:** ¡Qué más pudo pedir! - What else could you ask for! / a esa hora - at that time / a veces - at times / así que - so, therefore / bastante - quite, fairly / cerca de - near / colectivo - bus / creo que - I think that... / en cualquier lugar/lado - anywhere / en ese sentido - in that sense / en general - in general / la mayoría de - most / la verdad que - actually, the truth is that... / picante - spicy / por - because of / por - by / propio de - typical of / recién - just, only / sin ningún problema - without any problem **Multiple Choice:** 1. a[8-10] 2. d[7] 3. d **Vocabulary:** 1. parecido a 2. picante 3. despierto 4. despierto 5. avenida 6. lleno de 7. chico 8. sucio 9. amigable 10. llevarse bien 11. tratar de 12. almacén 13. clima 14. estar apurado 15. tránsito 16. subte 17. conurbano **Translate:** 1. a[4] Buenos Aires is the most Europe-like city. 2. de[14] La Plata is a city near Buenos Aires. 3. despierta[17] The city is awake the entire day (24/7). 4. que[23] Buenos Aires is smaller than New York. 5. de[30] The city is full of people in a hurry. 6. distintos tipos[39] There are different types of people.

La Cultura

El Fútbol en Costa Rica

Laura (Costa Rica)
574 words (142 wpm)
🔘 19

True or False

1. The Costa Rica soccer team managed to qualify to compete in the World Gold Cup.   T ☐ F ☐
2. Costa Ricans were sure their team would win.   T ☐ F ☐
3. The Costa Rican team managed to win the first match.   T ☐ F ☐
4. During the competition, everybody was kind and friendly.   T ☐ F ☐
5. Soccer has a minimal influence on Costa Ricans.   T ☐ F ☐

Expressions

de repente	at least
de verdad	it turns out that
el año pasado	last year
empatados	never mind
la gente se pone la camiseta	Oh my God
le ganamos a Italia	people wear t-shirts
meter un gol	really
no importa	simply
nos apoyamos	suddenly
por Dios	tied
por lo menos	to go nuts
quedarse callado	to score a goal
resulta que	to shut up
sencillamente	unprecedented
sin precedentes	we beat Italy
volverse loco	we support each other

Multiple Choice

1. According to Laura, Costa Ricans show support for their teams by ___ and ___.

    a. going to the stadium
    b. posting on social media
    c. painting their faces
    d. naming their children after players

2. "Cenicienta" (Cinderella) was the nickname that ___.

    a. the Costa Ricans gave Uruguay
    b. the Brazilians gave the Costa Ricans
    c. the Italians gave the Costa Ricans
    d. the Costa Ricans gave England

3. An idiomatic term for Costa Ricans is ___.

    a. costinos   b. tacos   c. ricos   d. ticos

Text

El fútbol en Costa Rica, y en general… general, en toda la región Latinoamericana, es algo que se vive con mucha pasión.	1	Soccer in Costa Rica, and in general… general in Latin America, is something that people are really passionate about.
La gente apoya muchísimo a sus equipos:	2	People very much support their teams:
la gente va a los estadios,	3	they go to the stadium,
se pone las camisetas de los colores,	4	they wear t-shirts with their team colors,
se pone maquillaje en la cara,	5	people paint their faces,
o sea, es de verdad algo que se vive con mucha pasión, el fútbol.	6	I mean, soccer is really something that people are passionate about.
Y bueno, lo que pasó el año pasado en el mundial de Brasil 2014 fue algo sin precedentes,	7	And well, what happened last year in the 2014 Football World Cup in Brazil was something unprecedented;
o sea, sin palabras lo que pasó en éste país.	8	that is, there are no words to describe what happened in this country.
Resulta que bueno, ahí con algunas dificultades, logramos clasificar entre los equipos para ir a participar al mundial.	9	It wasn't easy, but we [Costa Rica] managed to qualify among the countries competing in the World Cup.
Ya eso fue un gran logro y celebramos mucho,	10	This was already a great achievement, and we really celebrated,
y la gente estaba contenta.	11	and people were happy.
Y bueno, llegó el día en que hacen como la rifa de los países como los acomodan en los equipos	12	Then the day arrived when they do the raffle to accommodate all teams in different groups
para ver con quienes son los primeros que nos toca enfrentarnos.	13	to find out who we'd be up against first.
Y resulta que nos toca contra Italia, Inglaterra y Uruguay.	14	And it turns out we were up against Italy, England, and Uruguay.
O sea, todo el mundo estaba tan triste, tan deprimido, como decimos, tan ahuevados,	15	I mean, everybody was so upset, so depressed [about this], [or] as we say, "ahuevados" (gobsmacked),
porque por Dios, o sea Costa Rica, que es un equipo pequeño, que ahí va poco a poco, nos toca contra Italia, Inglaterra y Uruguay, o sea tres mega equipazos.	16	because, oh my God, this means Costa Rica, such a small team, having all this hard time [just to classify], had to play against Italy, England, and Uruguay, three mega super teams.
Así que bueno, todos estábamos como: ¡Ay para qué ir, entonces el mundial qué feo!	17	So, we were all like, "Oh, why bother going! To hell with the World Cup!"
Y bueno los jugadores decían: No importa, vamos a ir a darnos con todo,	18	But then the players said, "It doesn't matter. We are going to do our best,
vamos a ir a entregarnos a jugar con todas las fuerzas, verdad.	19	play with all we have, all our strength, of course."
Bueno, resulta que ya llega el primer partido contra Uruguay:	20	Okay, then the first match arrives, against Uruguay:
Tres a uno. ¡Ganamos! ¡Le ganamos a Uruguay!	21	3-1. We won! We beat Uruguay!
Bueno, ese país se volvió loco.	22	And this country went nuts.

La gente salía a las calles, celebrando, todo el mundo súper feliz.	23	People went out onto the streets, celebrating, everybody extremely happy.
¡Wow¡ ¡Le ganamos a Uruguay tres a uno!	24	Wow! We beat Uruguay 3-1!
Segundo partido, Italia uno - cero. Le ganamos a los italianos.	25	Second game, Italy: 1-0. We beat them, the Italians.
Esos italianos ¿saben cómo nos decían a nosotros? ¡Cenicienta!	26	You know what those Italians were calling us before the game? Cinderella!
Éramos la cenicienta del equipo.	27	We were the Cinderella team.
Uno - cero para que se queden callados los Italianos, ¡les ganamos!	28	1-0 got the Italians to shut up. We beat you!
Y luego contra Inglaterra cero - cero.	29	Then England 0-0.
No pudieron meternos ningún gol.	30	They couldn't score a single goal against us.
Bueno, ese país se volvió loco.	31	Well, this country really went crazy.
La gente salió a las calles, la gente celebraba, la gente gritaba, todo el mundo con banderas.	32	People were on the streets; people were celebrating; people were shouting, everyone with flags.
Pasamos a la siguiente ronda contra Grecia uno a uno empatados.	33	Then we went into the second round against Greece tying 1-1.
Y logramos pasar a la siguiente ronda.	34	And we passed to the next round.
O sea, para explicarles por qué fue que escogí este tema.	35	You know, I want to explain why I chose this subject.
Es porque simple y sencillamente nada, nunca, ningún acontecimiento había logrado unir más a un pueblo que esto.	36	It's because there had simply never been anything, any event that managed to bring a people together as this event did.
O sea, la gente se abrazaba, la gente salía a las calles, la gente andaba feliz.	37	I mean, people were hugging each other; people were on the streets; people were going around happy.
Dicen que la gente trabajaba con todas las ganas del mundo.	38	They say that people worked with all the enthusiasm in the world.
La gente se olvidó de repente por unos veintidós días de sus problemas.	39	People suddenly forgot their problems for 22 days.
La gente solo hablaba de fútbol,	40	Everybody just talked about soccer,
y todo el mundo estaba tranquilo, todo el mundo.	41	and everybody was calm. Everybody.
Entonces, de verdad que eso parece mentira	42	Indeed, as unreal as it may seem,
pero un evento deportivo así logró unir a todo un pueblo.	43	but a sporting event managed to unite an entire people.
Y logró hacer que todo un pueblo, por lo que duró el mundial o por lo menos hasta donde logramos llegar...	44	And it succeeded in making a whole country, during the World Cup, or at least for as long as we were still in [the competition]...
la gente fue feliz, la gente sonreía en las calles, la gente era amable.	45	people were happy; people were smiling in the streets, people were kind.
Fue muy bonito, o sea, uno de repente de verdad se identificaba.	46	It was beautiful, really, to feel that you belonged.
O sea, sos tico, yo soy tico.	47	You know, you are Costa Rican; I am Costa Rican.

Tenemos la misma camiseta, nos apoyamos:	48	We have the same t-shirt, we support each other:
mirá te hago este favor, mirá te... fue muy bonito.	49	Look, I can do you this favor, look... it was really nice.
Así que el soccer o el fútbol de verdad que tiene una gran influencia en las personas en Costa Rica	50	So, soccer, or football, has a really big influence on people in Costa Rica.
¡¡¡OEOEOEOEEEE TICOOOOSSS TICOOOOOSS!!!	51	OEOEOEOEEEE TICOOOOSSS TICOOOOOSS!!!

Vocabulary

1. team[2] _____
2. makeup[5] _____
3. to manage to do[9] _____
4. achievement[10] _____
5. against[14] _____
6. everybody[15] _____
7. to win[21] _____
8. flag[32] _____
9. the next[33] _____
10. to choose[35] _____
11. event[36] _____
12. to hug[37] _____
13. to forget[39] _____
14. lie[42] _____
15. to smile[45] _____
16. to do a favor[49] _____

Translate

1. Lo que pasó el año pasado *fue / era* algo sin precedentes.
2. Eso fue un gran *logro / logramiento* para el equipo.
3. El país se *volvió / fue* loco.
4. Le ganamos *a / hacia* Uruguay.
5. Te *hago / doy* ese favor.
6. El fútbol *de / en* verdad tiene una gran influencia en las personas en Costa Rica.

notes

True or False: 1. T[9] 2. F[15] 3. T[21] 4. T[36] 5. F[50] **Expressions:** de repente - suddenly / de verdad - really / el año pasado - last year / empatados - tied / la gente se pone la camiseta - people wear t-shirts / le ganamos a Italia - we beat Italy / meter un gol - to score a goal / no importa - never mind / nos apoyamos - we support each other / por Dios - Oh my God / por lo menos - at least / quedarse callado - to shut up / resulta que - it turns out that / sencillamente - simply / sin precedentes - unprecedented / volverse loco - to go nuts **Multiple Choice:** 1. a[3], c[5] 2. c[26] 3. d[51] **Vocabulary:** 1. equipo 2. maquillage 3. lograr 4. logro 5. contra 6. todo el mundo 7. ganar 8. bandera 9. la siguiente 10. escoger 11. acotecimiento 12. abrazar 13. olvidar 14. mentira 15. sonreír 16. hacer un favor **Translate:** 1. fue[7] What happened last year was something unprecedented. 2. logro[10] That was a great achievement for the team. 3. volvió[22] The country went crazy. 4. a[24] We beat Uruguay. 5. hago[49] I'll do that favor for you. 6. de[50] Soccer has a really significant influence on people in Costa Rica.

El Turismo en Perú

Jorge (Peru)
419 words (116 wpm)
🔊 20

True or False

1. Peru has two of the seven wonders of the world. T☐ F☐
2. The most popular area of Peru among tourists is the south. T☐ F☐
3. There are many famous beaches in the south of Peru. T☐ F☐
4. People go to Trujillo to go surfing. T☐ F☐
5. In Mancora, there's nothing to do but relax. T☐ F☐

Expressions

a lo lago de	do not miss the chance
al llegar	extraordinary
deja de ser	it is due to
eso se debe a	it is no longer
fuera de lo común	on the other end
no pierdan la oportunidad	throughout
por el otro lado	upon arriving

Multiple Choice

1. Peru has repeatedly won the award for best ___.

    a. hospitality at resorts
    b. surfing destination in the world
    c. tourist destination in South America
    d. culinary destination

2. The city of Pisco is well known for the local production of ___.

    a. coffee
    b. peaches
    c. liquor
    d. flowers

3. Arequipa is called the ___ City.

    a. Green
    b. White
    c. Blue
    d. Red

Text

El turismo en el Perú es un tema muy interesante, muy amplio.	1	Tourism in Peru is a very interesting, broad topic.
Yo comenzaría con que el país ha ganado mucho reconocimiento en los últimos años por varios cosas.	2	I'd begin with [the fact] that the country has gained much recognition in recent years for several things.
La primera para mi seria que ahora nosotros tenemos una de la siete nuevas maravillas del mundo, eh… la cual se llama Machu Picchu.	3	The first for me would be that we now have one of the seven new wonders of the world, uh… which is called Machu Picchu.
Eh… y la otra, como buen cocinero que soy, sería la comida, ya que el Perú ha ganado el premio a mejor destino culinario por cuatro años consecutivos,	4	Uh… and the other, being the good cook that I am, would be the food, as Peru has won the award four years running for best culinary destination,

cosa que se debe a la gran variedad de productos que cosechamos a lo largo de año, por la gran variedad de microclimas que hay en la diferentes regiones del Perú.	5	which is due to the variety of products we harvest throughout the year because of the variety of microclimates that exist in different regions of Peru.
Si yo fuera turista, mi primera parada en… en el Perú sería Lima, nuestra ciudad capital.	6	If I were a tourist, my first stop in Peru would be Lima, our capital city.
Eh… normalmente lo que hacen los turistas, al llegar… una vez llegan a Lima, es recorrer el sur del Perú,	7	Uh… normally what tourists do, upon arriving… once they arrive in Lima, is to tour the south of Peru,
ya que al sur del Perú tenemos, eh… a cuatro horas de Lima, tenemos Ica.	8	because in southern Peru we have, uh… four hours from Lima, we have Ica.
Muy, muy cerca de Ica tenemos el único oasis natural de toda América, que se llama Huacachina.	9	Very, very close to Ica, we have the only natural oasis in all of the Americas, which is called Huacachina.
Eh… tenemos la ciudad de Pisco, que es muy conocida por eh… nuestro aguardiente nacional, que es el Pisco del mismo nombre.	10	Uh… we have the city of Pisco, which is well known for uh… our national liquor, which is the Pisco, of the same name.
Más al sur tenemos la Ciudad Blanca de Arequipa, muy conocida por sus em… por sus paisajes, por el volcán Misti que tenemos.	11	Further south, we have the "White City" of Arequipa, well known for its um… for his landscape, for the Misti volcano we have [there].
La comida arequipeña es muy, muy, muy, fuera de lo común.	12	Arequipan food is very, very, very extraordinary.
Es demasiado, demasiado deliciosa.	13	It's very, very delicious.
Em… un poco más al sur tenemos Cusco, que es la ciudad donde se encuentra Machu Picchu.	14	Um… a little further south, we have Cusco, which is the city where Machu Picchu is found.
Em… ese es el principal atractivo turístico que tenemos en el Perú, em… bueno, al sur del Perú.	15	Um… that's the main attraction we have in Peru, um… well, in southern Peru.
Por el otro lado, al norte tenemos variedad de playas.	16	On the other hand, to the north, we have a variety of beaches.
Eh… tenemos la ciudad de Trujillo, que es em… el destino turístico para el surf.	17	Uh… we have to Trujillo, which is um… the touristic destination for surfing.
Más al norte tenemos Máncora, que es un pueblo al norte de la ciudad de Piura.	18	Further north, we have Mancora, a town to the north of the city of Piura.
Es muy… muy conocida por el… por el ambiente fiestero que puede llegar a tener.	19	It's very… very well known for the… for the party atmosphere that it can have.
Es muy pequeño, pero la gente sabe como divertirse.	20	It's very small, but people know how to have fun.
Un poco más al sur tenemos Tumbes, que es em… ya em… que deja de ser costa y pasa a ser más esto em… selva.	21	A little further south, we have Tumbes, which is um… um… which is no longer the coast and becomes more uh… um… rainforest.
La selva del Perú es muy, muy grande.	22	Peru's rainforest is very, very big.
Tenemos reservas naturales muy grandes.	23	We have very large nature reserves.
Eh… lo que yo diría como peruano es em…	24	Uh… what I would say as Peruvian is um…

si alguna vez tienen la oportunidad de conocer el Perú, esto… no pierdan la oportunidad,	25	if you have the opportunity to visit Peru sometime, um… do not miss that chance,
porque palabras eh… faltan para describir la experiencia eh… que pueden llegar a vivir.	26	because words uh… fail to describe the experience uh… you can come to experience.
Se los recomiendo.	27	I recommend it.

Vocabulary

1. wide[1] _____
2. wonder[3] _____
3. to harvest[5] _____
4. liquor[10] _____
5. landscape[11] _____
6. town[18] _____
7. festive[19] _____
8. rainforest[21] _____
9. to become[21] _____
10. sometime[25] _____

Translate

1. Yo comenzaría con que el país ha ganado mucho reconocimiento en *los / -* últimos años por varios cosas.
2. Cosechamos una gran variedad de productos *a lo largo / durante* de año.
3. Si yo *fuera / estuviera* turista, mi primera parada en el Perú sería Lima, nuestra ciudad capital.
4. La comida arequipeña es muy fuera *de lo / del* común.
5. La ciudad es muy conocida *por / para* el ambiente fiestero que puede llegar a tener.
6. Un poco más al sur tenemos Tumbes, que deja *de / a* ser costa y pasa a ser más selva.

notes

True or False: 1. F[3] 2. T[7] 3. F[16] 4. T[17] 5. F[19-20] **Expressions:** a lo lago de - throughout / al llegar - upon arriving / deja de ser - it is no longer / eso se debe a - it is due to / fuera de lo común - extraordinary / no pierdan la oportunidad - do not miss the chance / por el otro lado - on the other end **Multiple Choice:** 1. d[4] 2. c[10] 3. b[11] **Vocabulary:** 1. amplio 2. maravilla 3. cosechar 4. aguardiente 5. paisaje 6. pueblo 7. fiestero 8. selva 9. pasar a ser 10. alguna vez **Translate:** 1. los[2] I would begin with [the fact] that the country has gained a lot of recognition in recent years for several things. 2. a lo largo[5] We harvest a wide variety of products throughout the year. 3. fuera[6] If I were a tourist, my first stop in Peru would be Lima, our capital city. 4. de lo[12] Arequipan food is very extraordinary. 5. por[19] The city is well known for the party environment it can have. 6. de[21] A little further south, we have Tumbes, which ceases to be the coast and becomes more jungle.

Espanglish

Sandra (Mexico)
429 words (123 wpm)
○ 21

True or False

1. Sandra defines Spanglish as a mixture of English and Spanish. T☐ F☐
2. Spanglish is used by many young people in Mexico. T☐ F☐
3. Mudarse is the Spanglish word for 'to move.' T☐ F☐
4. The word pa'tras is a result of the influence by the use of the English word 'back.' T☐ F☐
5. Sandra mentions that she uses Spanglish in her daily speech. T☐ F☐

Expressions

¿Qué es esto?	by way of
¿verdad?	I'm going to talk about
alguien	instead of
en lugar de	is commonly known as
por medio de	mainly
principalmente	right?
se conoce comúnmente como	someone
suelen tener	try to adapt
tratan de adaptar	usually have
voy a hablar de	What is this?

Multiple Choice

1. Sandra mentions Spanglish words for ___ and ___.

   a. truck   c. movie
   b. literally d. support

2. Which of the following is true?

   a. Sandra expresses her disapproval of the use of Spanglish.
   b. Sandra says she enjoys using Spanish words.
   c. Sandra thinks Spanglish words should be included in the dictionary.
   d. Sandra does not give her opinion of the phenomenon of Spanglish.

3. Sandra implies that Spanish speakers in the United States often ___.

   a. have an American English accent
   b. misspell many Spanish words
   c. cannot understand people from Mexico
   d. misunderstand other Spanish speakers

Text

Les voy a hablar del español que se habla aquí en los Estados Unidos.	1	I am going to tell you about the Spanish that is spoken here in the United States.
Muchas personas aquí en Estados Unidos hablan el español,	2	Many people here in the United States speak Spanish,
principalmente personas que viven en frontera con... con México	3	mainly people that live by the border with... with Mexico.

Estas personas han adquirido el español por medio de su familia, de sus papás.	4	These people have acquired Spanish by way of their family, from their parents.
Y entonces han creado una variedad del español muy interesante que es diferente al español estándar.	5	So, they have created a very interesting variety of Spanish that is different from standard Spanish.
Es lo que se conoce comúnmente como el "Spanglish".	6	It's what is commonly known as "Spanglish."
¿Qué es esto? Es… el español aquí es una mezcla ¿verdad?	7	What is this? It's… Spanish here is a mix, right?
La…las personas hacen transferencias del inglés hacia el español,	8	The… people carry things over from English into Spanish,
y tratan de adaptar algunas palabras, algunas expresiones.	9	and they try to adapt some words, some expressions.
Algunos ejemplos pueden ser por ejemplo la palabra "mudarse", que en inglés es "to move".	10	Some examples could be, for example, the word "mudarse," which in English is "to move."
La gente aquí diría "vamos a movernos" en lugar de "vamos a mudarnos" ¿ok?	11	People here would say "vamos a movernos" instead of "vamos a mudarnos" ok?
Otra palabra que puedo pensar es la palabra em… "apoyar", que en inglés es "to support".	12	Another word I can think of is the word um… "apoyar," which in English is "to support."
Entonces la gente dice vam-… "yo te soporto" en lugar de "yo te apoyo" ¿verdad?	13	So people say… "yo te soporto" instead of "yo te apoyo," right?
También hay otras palabras que, del inglés, forman una nueva palabra,	14	There are also some words that, from English, they create a new word,
y la ocupan como si fuera español.	15	and they use it as if it were Spanish.
Tal es el ejemplo de la palabra "troca", que viene del inglés "truck".	16	An example of this is the word "troca," which comes from the English "truck."
Y utilizan esta palabra en lugar de decir "camioneta".	17	And they use this word instead of saying "camioneta."
O la palabra "carpeta" que viene del inglés "carpet" y la utilizan en lugar de "alfombra".	18	Or the word "carpeta," which comes from English, and they use it instead of "alfombra."
También hay… hay muchas expresiones que utilizan que dicen "pa' tras".	19	There's also…. there are many expressions they use where they say "pa'tras."
Por ejemplo, si dices a alguien "yo te devuelvo la llamada" ¿verdad? que significa "I call you back".	20	For example, If you say to someone "yo te devuelvo la llamada" right? That means "I call you back."
Estas personas van a decir eh… "yo te hablo para atrás" ¿no?	21	These people will say uh… "yo te hablo para atrás," right?
O en lugar de… de "regresar"… "voy a regresar", "I'll go back", dicen "yo voy a ir para atrás".	22	Or instead of… of "regresar"… "voy a regresar," "I'll go back," they say "voy a ir para atras."
Eh… también existen otras… se hacen como traducciones literales de expresiones.	23	Uh… there are also… they make, like, literal translations of expressions.
Por ejemplo, en inglés dices "How did you like the movie?";	24	For example, in English, you say, "How did you like the movie?"
en español dirías "¿Te gustó la película?"	25	In Spanish you would say "¿Te gustó la película?"

Pero entonces ellos van a decir "¿Cómo te gustó la película?" ¿verdad?	26	But then, they will say "¿Cómo te gustó la película?" right?
Otro... otra cosa que pasa con las personas que adquieren el español aquí en los Estados Unidos es que no saben escribir el español.	27	Another... another thing that happens with people that acquire Spanish here in the United States is that they don't know how to write in Spanish.
Lo saben hablar, pero nunca lo aprendieron a escribir.	28	They know how to speak, but they never learned to write it.
Entonces eh... aquí las personas suelen tener muy mala ortografía porque escriben el español como lo escuchan,	29	So uh... people here usually have very poor spelling because they write Spanish as they hear it,
pero nunca es... este... aprendieron a escribirlo.	30	but they never uh... uh... learned how to write it.
Entonces eh... van a escribir palabras que deben de ir con Y [ye], las van a escribir con LL [doble ele].	31	So, uh... they will write words that should be [spelled] with Y, they'll write them with LL.
van a cambiar la C [ce] por S [ese], eh... la V [uve] en lugar de B [be grande] ¿verdad?	32	They will change C to S, uh... V instead of B, right?
Em... solamente van a... a... a... escribirlo como ellos lo escuchan.	33	Um... they're just going to... to... write it as they hear it.

Vocabulary

1. mainly[3] _____
2. border[3] _____
3. to acquire[4] _____
4. parents[4] _____
5. standard[5] _____
6. mix[7] _____
7. to transfer[8] _____
8. to move[10] _____
9. to use[15] _____
10. carpet[18] _____

Translate

1. Estas personas han adquirido el español *por / a medio de* sus papás.
2. Las personas hacen transferencias / *transferimientos* del inglés hacia el español.
3. Toman palabras ingleses y las ocupan como si *fueran / sean* españolas.
4. Utilizan esta palabra *en / al* lugar de decir "camioneta".
5. Esas personas nunca *aprendieron / aprendan* a escribirlo.
6. Solamente van a *escribirlo / lo escribir* como ellos lo escuchan.

notes

True or False: 1. T[6-7] 2. F[2-4] 3. F[10-11] 4. T[19-22] 5. F **Expressions:** ¿Qué es esto? - What is this? / ¿verdad? - right? / alguien - someone / en lugar de - instead of / por medio de - by way of / principalmente - mainly / se conoce comúnmente como - is commonly known as / suelen tener - usually have / tratan de adaptar - try to adapt / voy a hablar de - I'm going to talk about **Multiple Choice:** 1. a[16], d[12-13] 2. d 3. b[29] **Vocabulary:** 1. principalmente 2. frontera 3. adquirir 4. papás 5. estándar 6. mezcla 7. hacer transferencias 8. mudarse 9. ocupar algo 10. alfombra **Translate:** 1. por[4] These people have acquired Spanish from their parents. 2. transferencias[8] People carry things over from English to Spanish. 3. fueran[15] They take English words and use them as if they were Spanish. 4. en[17] They use this word instead of saying "truck." 5. aprendieron[30] Those people never learned to write it. 6. escribirlo[33] They are only going to write it to write as they hear it.

La Religión en Honduras

José (Honduras)
303 words (140 wpm)
🔊 22

True or False

1. The first mass after Columbus's discovery of the Americas was celebrated in Trujillo.   T ☐   F ☐
2. Hondurans, in general, are not very religious.   T ☐   F ☐
3. Evangelical Christian communities are well-established in Honduras.   T ☐   F ☐
4. The number of churches is gradually decreasing because the young generation has no fear of God.   T ☐   F ☐
5. In Honduras, government representatives are not allowed to take part in public religious events.   T ☐   F ☐

Expressions

desde pequeños	from a young age
en honor a	in honor of
es parte de	is moving toward
ha crecido bastante	it has grown considerably
hay muy pocos	it has to do with
luego	it is part of
se está moviendo hacia	then
son basadas en	there are very few
tiene que ver con	they're based on

Multiple Choice

1. José mentions that about 70% of Hondurans ___.
    a. have been baptized
    b. are Mormons, Jehovah's Witnesses, or Jews
    c. don't go to church on a regular basis
    d. *none of the above*

2. The feast of Our Lady of Suyapa is celebrated on ___.
    a. January 2   b. February 2   c. January 12   d. February 12

3. Father's Day is celebrated in honor of ___.
    a. Saint David   b. Saint Nicholas   c. Saint Joseph   d. Saint Francis

Text

La religión en mi país es una… es una idiosincrasia.	1	Religion in my country is a… is an idiosyncrasy.
Es una… es algo que está bien arraigado en nuestro pueblo.	2	It's a… it's something that is well-rooted in our people.
De hecho, la ciudad de Trujillo es la ciudad donde se celebró la primera misa.	3	In fact, the city of Trujillo is the city where the first Mass was celebrated.

Cuando Cristóbal Colón vino a América, aquí en Trujillo fue donde se celebró la primera misa.	4	When Christopher Columbus came to America, here in Trujillo was where the first Mass was celebrated.
La mayoría de las personas son católicas.	5	Most people are Catholic.
Creo que aproximadamente el setenta por ciento de la población es católica.	6	I think about 70% of the population is Catholic.
Luego tenemos cristianos evangélicos.	7	Then we have evangelical Christians.
También tenemos mormones; tenemos Testigos de Jehová.	8	We also have Mormons; we have Jehovah's Witnesses.
Tenemos... y otros... Religiones protestantes también tenemos aquí en nuestro país.	9	We have... and others... We also have Protestant religions here in our country.
Hay muy pocos judíos, pero sí los hay.	10	There are very few Jews, but there are some.
Y la religión es parte de nuestra historia.	11	And religion is part of our history.
Es parte de lo que somos, de nuestro legado.	12	It is part of who we are, our legacy.
Tenemos celebraciones o feriados que tienen que ver con la religión.	13	We celebrations and holidays that have to do with religion.
Por ejemplo, el dos de febrero se celebra el día de la Virgen de Suyapa, que es un feriado.	14	For example, the feast of Our Lady of Suyapa, which is a holiday, is celebrated on February 2.
El Día del Padre se celebra en honor a San José, que también es un feriado nacional.	15	Father's Day is celebrated in honor of St. Joseph, and this is also a national holiday.
Y hay otras celebraciones que son basadas en asuntos religiosos.	16	And there are other celebrations that are based on religious affairs.
La gente aquí en Honduras es muy religiosa;	17	People here in Honduras are very religious;
van a los templos, van a las iglesias.	18	They go to temples, go to churches.
El movimiento cristiano evangélico es un movimiento que ha crecido bastante en el país.	19	The evangelical Christian movement is a movement that has grown considerably in the country.
Tenemos templos grandísimos de cristianos evangélicos.	20	We have huge evangelical Christian churches.
Las iglesias están creciendo.	21	The churches are growing.
Hay mucha gente que cada día se está moviendo hacia las iglesias, hacia la religión,	22	There are many people who are moving toward the churches, to religion, every day,
porque pues es algo que se nos enseña desde pequeños, ¿no?	23	because it is something we are taught from a young age, right?
A tener temor de Dios, en el caso de los cristianos evangélicos y de los católicos y pues todas las iglesias protestantes.	24	To have a fear of God, in the case of evangelical Christians and Catholics, and for all Protestant churches.
Desde pequeño se inculca, ¿no?, el que hay un Dios.	25	It's instilled from an early age that there is a God, right?
El aspecto religioso está muy arraigado en nuestro pueblo.	26	The religious dimension is deeply rooted in our people.
Aun el presidente ha hecho actos donde hacen oraciones a Dios.	27	Even the president has participated in ceremonies in which they pray to God.
Hacen invocaciones en estadios, en eventos, que organiza la Iglesia.	28	They make invocations in stadiums, in events organized by the Church.

Vocabulary

1. idiosyncrasy[1] _____
2. rooted[2] _____
3. mass[4] _____
4. Catholic[5] _____
5. evangelical Christians[7] _____
6. mormons[8] _____
7. Jehovah's witnesses[8] _____
8. Protestants[9] _____
9. Jews[10] _____
10. legacy[12] _____
11. holidays[13] _____
12. Father's day[15] _____
13. fear of God[24] _____
14. to instill[25] _____

Translate

1. Fue cuando Cristóbal Colón *vino / vinió* a América, aquí en Trujillo.
2. Tenemos celebraciones o feriados que tienen *que / a* ver con la religión.
3. El Día del Padre se celebra en honor *a / de* un Santo y también es un feriado nacional.
4. Hay otras celebraciones que son basadas *en / de* asuntos religiosos.
5. La gente se está moviendo *hacia / hasta* las iglesias.
6. Es algo que *nos se / se nos* enseña desde pequeños.

notes

True or False: 1. F[3] 2. F[17] 3. T[19] 4. F[22] 5. F[27] **Expressions:** desde pequeños - from a young age / en honor a - in honor of / es parte de - it is part of / ha crecido bastante - it has grown considerably / hay muy pocos - there are very few / luego - then / se está moviendo hacia - is moving toward / son basadas en - they're based on / tiene que ver con - it has to do with **Multiple Choice:** 1. d[6] 2. b[14] 3. c[15] **Vocabulary:** 1. idiosincrasia 2. arraigado 3. misa 4. católico 5. cristianos evangélicos 6. Mormones 7. Testigos de Jehová 8. protestantes 9. judíos 10. legado 11. feriados 12. Día del Padre 13. temor de Dios 14. inculcar **Translate:** 1. vino[4] It was when Christopher Columbus came to America, here in Trujillo. 2. que[13] We have celebrations or holidays that have to do with religion. 3. a[15] Father's Day is celebrated in honor of a Saint and is also a national holiday. 4. en[16] There are other celebrations that are based on religious matters. 5. hacia[22] People are moving toward the churches. 6. nos se[23] It is something that is taught from a young age.

El Cine Español

Francisco (Spain)
295 words (127 wpm) 💿 23

True or False

1. Cinema first arrived in Spain decades after its diffusion in the other European countries. T☐ F☐
2. Francisco mentions his favorite actor and director. T☐ F☐
3. The erotic genre arose after the death of Franco. T☐ F☐
4. In Spain, cinema came to a truly professional level in the 1960's. T☐ F☐
5. Spanish movie directors won Oscar awards in the 1980's. T☐ F☐

Expressions

actualmente	currently
como contrapunto a	definitely
definitivamente	in response to
incluyendo	including
muy conocido	occurs
poco después	shortly after
protagonizado por	starring
se produce	well known

Multiple Choice

1. Spanish cinema arose in the ___.
    a. late eighteenth century   c. early twentieth century
    b. late nineteenth century   d. *none of the above*

2. ___ was a filmmaker, actor, and writer.
    a. Carlos Saura   c. Javier Bardem
    b. Fernán Gomez   d. Luis García Berlanga

3. During the latter years of the Franco dictatorship, Spanish cinematographic production was mostly ___.
    a. dramatic   b. historical   c. erotic   d. humorous

Text

El cine en España comenzó a desarrollarse a finales del siglo XIX, mil ochocientos ochenta y tantos,	1	Cinema in Spain began to develop in the late nineteenth century, eighteen eighty-something,
poco después de que fuese inventado en Francia por los hermanos Lumiére.	2	shortly after it was invented in France by the Lumiere brothers.
El cine español ha pasado por muchas épocas,	3	Spanish cinema has gone through many periods,
incluyendo la guerra civil española y la dictadura de Franco en la cual también se hizo cine,	4	including the Spanish civil war and the Franco dictatorship, during which movies were also made,

lo que ha afectado, pues, al desarrollo del cine español.	5	which has affected, well, the development of Spanish cinema.
En España nacieron cineastas de gran prestigio en el siglo XX (veinte),	6	In Spain, prestigious filmmakers were born in the twentieth century,
como Luis Buñuel (famoso por sus primeros filmes surrealistas, en colaboración, entre otros, con Salvador Dalí, el gran genio español del surrealismo).	7	like Luis Buñuel (famous for his early Surrealist films, collaborating with, among others, Salvador Dali, the great Spanish genius of Surrealism).
También Luis García Berlanga, Carlos Saura o Fernando Fernán Gómez. Este último, también fue un actor y escritor de gran prestigio.	8	Also Luis Garcia Berlanga, Carlos Saura, or Fernando Fernan Gomez. The latter was also an actor and writer of great prestige.
Durante los años sesenta, coincidiendo con la apertura de España al turismo internacional,	9	In the sixties, coinciding with the opening of Spain to international tourism,
y donde la dictadura tuvo sus años menos duros, se produce una explosión, un boom del cine español.	10	when the dictatorship had become less hardline, an explosion, a boom in Spanish cinema, occurs.
Era un cine humorístico, costumbrista, folklórico, básicamente de entretenimiento,	11	It was humorous cinema, with a local flavor, basically just entertaining,
protagonizado pues por estrellas de la canción, como Manolo Escobar o Marisol,	12	starring singing stars, such as Manolo Escobar or Marisol,
pero del que surgieron grandísimos actores como José Luis López Vázquez o Alfredo Landa, y que fue escuela para muchos directores.	13	but out of which great actors like Jose Luis Lopez Vazquez or Alfredo Landa emerged, and it was an education [schooling] for many directors.
Durante la transición española, después de la muerte del dictador, surgen, pues, el género erótico, como contrapunto a muchos años de censura.	14	During the Spanish transition, after the dictator's death, well, the erotic genre arises, in response to years of censorship,
y otro tipo de cine más comprometido que toca temas sociales, e incluso temas políticos.	15	as well as other kinds of more committed cinema that focus on social themes, including political themes.
Después de los años ochenta, el cine español comienza a entrar en su madurez,	16	After the eighties, Spanish cinema begins to enter maturity,
y se convierte en una industria consolidada y definitivamente profesional,	17	and it becomes a consolidated and definitely professional industry,
con directores que ganan Oscars de Hollywood, como José Luis Garci, Fernando Trueba, Amenábar,	18	with directors winning Hollywood Oscars, such as José Luis Garci, Fernando Trueba, Amenabar,
o Almodóvar, que es el más famoso actualmente de los directores españoles,	19	or Almodóvar, who is currently the most famous of Spanish directors,
y actores y actrices internacionales como Penélope Cruz, Antonio Banderas o Javier Bardem, muy conocidos mundialmente.	20	and international actors and actresses such as Penelope Cruz, Antonio Banderas, and Javier Bardem, well known worldwide.

Vocabulary

1. to develop[1] _____
2. to go through[3] _____
3. to affect[5] _____
4. filmmaker[6] _____
5. opening[9] _____
6. starring[12] _____
7. committed[15] _____
8. maturity[16] _____
9. currently[19] _____
10. worldwide[20] _____

Translate

1. El cine en España *comenzó / comenció* a desarrollarse a finales del siglo XIX.
2. El cine español ha pasado *por / entre* muchas épocas.
3. Cuando la dictadura *tuvo / tenió* sus años menos duros, se produce un boom del cine español.
4. Era un cine protagonizado *por / de* estrellas de la canción.
5. Durante la transición española, después *de / -* la muerte de Franco, surgen otros generos.
6. El cine se convierte *en / a* una industria consolidada y definitivamente profesional.

notes

True or False: 1. F[2] 2. F 3. T[14] 4. F[16-17] 5. T[18] **Expressions:** actualmente - currently / como contrapunto a - in response to / definitivamente - definitely / incluyendo - including / muy conocido - well known / poco después - shortly after / protagonizado por - starring / se produce - occurs **Multiple Choice:** 1. b[1] 2. b[8] 3. d[10-11] **Vocabulary:** 1. desarrollarse 2. pasar por 3. afectar 4. cineasta 5. apertura 6. protagonizado por 7. comprometido 8. madurez 9. actualmente 10. mundialmente **Translate:** 1. comenzó[1] Cinema in Spain began to develop in the late 19th century. 2. por[3] Spanish cinema has gone through many periods. 3. tuvo[10] When the dictatorship had become less hardline, a boom in Spanish occurs. 4. por[12] It was a cinema starring singing stars. 5. de[14] During the Spanish transition, after the death of Franco, other genres arise. 6. en[17] Cinema becomes a consolidated and definitely professional industry.

Los Casamientos Argentinos

Florencia (Argentina)
657 words (156 wpm)
🔊 24

True or False

1. In Argentina, traditional weddings tend to be celebrated at nighttime. T ☐ F ☐
2. Florencia went to a wedding where the bride parachuted in. T ☐ F ☐
3. Food is an important part of traditional Argentinian weddings. T ☐ F ☐
4. Argentinian weddings are very long ceremonies. T ☐ F ☐
5. The married couple usually waits for their guests to go home before leaving on their honeymoon. T ☐ F ☐

Expressions

a veces	a bit more
al mediodía	a few years ago
antes	afterward, then
así que	all night
bueno	and so on
de noche	around, surrounding
después	at night
destacable	at noon
durante el día	back(ward)
en ese sentido	before
en forma abundante	even
en torno a	in abundance
hace unos años atrás	in that sense
hacia atrás	in the daytime
incluso	remarkable
lo más importante	so, therefore
toda la noche	sometimes
un poco más	the most important thing
usualmente	usually
y así	well

Multiple Choice

1. Which is true about the wedding Florencia tells us about?
    a. All of the guests wore country-style outfits.
    b. Several guests got food poisoning.
    c. The food was all locally produced and homemade.
    d. She caught the bride's bouquet.

2. Which <u>two</u> wedding traditions supposedly indicate who will be getting married next?
    a. catching the bride's bouquet
    b. taking a garter off the bride's leg
    c. being the last guest to leave
    d. finding a ring in the wedding cake

3. What does Florencia tell us is the most important thing at a wedding?
    a. the music   b. the food   c. the party games   d. the speeches

Text

¡Hola! Mi nombre es Florencia y soy de Buenos Aires, Argentina.	1	Hi! My name is Florencia, and I'm from Buenos Aires, Argentina.
En Buenos Aires los casamientos en general son de noche.	2	In Buenos Aires, weddings are generally at night.
Hace unos años atrás se empezó a poner de moda los casamientos de día,	3	A few years ago, daytime weddings started to come into style,
que usualmente se hace en las afueras de la ciudad.	4	and these usually take place outside of the city.
Y... en general el tema es un... un estilo campo, digamos.	5	And... in general, the theme is a... country style, let's say.
Fui a un casamiento hace unos años durante el día,	6	I went to a wedding a few years ago during the day,
y lo hicimos en... en un lugar bien... bien de campo,	7	and we did it in... in a very... very rural place,
con cosas con pan casero, con quesos caseros, toda producción del lugar,	8	with things with homemade bread, with homemade cheese, everything locally made,
y... y muy linda, muy rica la comida, muy lindo el lugar.	9	and... and really lovely, very rich food, a very nice place.
Y em... todo el casamiento fue en torno a lo campestre.	10	And um... the whole wedding was rural-themed.
Los novios llegaron en sulky, con los caballos.	11*	The couple arrived in a sulky, with horses.
Y... comimos carne asada y comimos distintos tipos de quesos que habían hecho ahí en el lugar.	12	And... we ate roasted meat, and we ate different types of cheese they had made there at the place.
Comenzó al mediodía con alguna picada.	13*	It began at noon with some "picada."
Después se hizo la ceremonia y luego eh... comimos en un lugar cerrado,	14	After that, the ceremony took place, and then uh... we ate in an enclosed area,
donde entre comidas se ponía música y se podía bailar,	15	where between food, they put on music, and you could dance,
y después sentarse de vuelta y comer un poco más y... y así.	16	and then sit down again and eat some more and... so on.
Lo mismo es de noche, también, los casamientos.	17	It's the same for nighttime weddings, too.
Hay distintos tipos de costumbres para los casamientos,	18	There are different types of customs for weddings,
pero los más em... lo más destacables, o los más comunes son:	19	but the most um... remarkable, or the most common are:
poner en la torta em... distintos tipos de dijes.	20	to put um... different types of charms in the cake.
Uno de ellos va a ser un anillo.	21	One of them is a ring.
Y cada dije está conectado a una cinta que sale hacia afuera de la torta.	22	And each charm is connected to a ribbon that comes out of the cake.
Entonces, bueno, todas las mujeres este... solteras lo que hacen es tirar de esta cinta.	23	Then, well, all the uh... single women, what they do is pull out this ribbon.
A veces lo hacen en la torta y otras veces en una copa aparte.	24	Sometimes they do on the cake and sometimes in a separate cup.

Pero la idea es que todas las mujeres solteras tiren de esa cinta,	25	But the idea is that all the single women pull on that ribbon,
y van a encontrarse con distintos dijes,	26	and they will find various charms,
pero la que se lleva el anillo es la que… es la próxima que se va a casar.	27	but the one with the ring is the one that… the next one to get married.
Lo mismo hacemos con el ramo:	28	We do the same with the bouquet:
la novia tira su ramo hacia atrás a un grupo de mujeres que se… se ubica atrás, que son solteras,	29	the bride throws her bouquet back to a group of women who… are back there, who are single,
y quién obtiene el ramo es la próxima que se va a casar.	30	and whoever gets the bouquet is the next to get married.
Después, está… hay otra costumbre que es eh… es cómo… se llama "el juego de la liga",	31	Then there's… there's another custom that is uh… it's like… it's called "the garter game,"
que es que una mujer… la novia, perdón, tiene una liga en la pierna,	32	in which a woman… the bride, excuse me, has a garter on her leg,
y el novio eh… se la saca, le saca la primera liga.	33	and the groom uh… takes it off her, takes the first garter off her.
Y después los mejores amigos del novio le sacan, con la mano, con los dientes o como sea, el resto de las ligas que la novia tiene entre… debajo su vestido.	34	And then the groom's best friends take off, using their hands, teeth, or whatever, the rest of the garters that the bride has between… under her dress.
Así que en ese sentido, bueno, es un momento para reírse y para disfrutar.	35	So, in that sense, well, it's a time to laugh and to enjoy oneself.
Lo más importante de un casamiento argentino es que haya comida,	36	The most important thing for an Argentinian wedding is that there be food,
que haya buena comida y en forma abundante.	37	that there be good food and in abundance.
Es una… todo gira en torno a la comida.	38	It's a… everything revolves around food.
Es una señal de que uno invita y está contento de que estén… de que están invitados.	39	It's a sign that one is inviting and is happy that… you are invited.
Otra cosa que sucede en los casamientos es que duran mucho tiempo.	40	Another thing that happens at weddings is that they last a long time.
Si son a la noche incluso pueden terminar con desayuno,	41	If they are at night, they may even end with breakfast,
y… así que duran toda… toda la noche.	42	and… so they last throughout the whole night.
Usualmente, cuando llegan los novios, se baila el vals, se pone un vals,	43	Usually, when the bride and groom get there, the waltz is danced, they put on waltz [music],
y los novios bailan con los padres,	44	and the couple dance with their parents,
y después, van acercándose los amigos y van bailando con distintos familiares y amigos.	45	and then closer friends come, and they go on dancing with various relatives and friends.
Después, eh… se termina con lo que se llama del carnaval carioca o baile carioca,	46*	Then, uh… they finish with what is called carioca carnival or carioca dance,
que es poner música brasilera y tirar papel picado, ponerse distintos sombreros,	47	which is putting on Brazilian music and throwing confetti, wearing different hats,

distintos tipos de cotillón donde la gente, bueno, se divierte un poco más.		different types of party favors, at which point people, well, have a bit more fun.
Los novios siempre… casi siempre se retiran antes terminar la fiesta,	48	The bride and groom always… almost always leave before the party is over,
en un momento de nadie los ve, nadie se entera,	49	when nobody sees them, nobody knows,
y es como que se van a escondidas de la fiesta.	50	and it's like they sneak away from the party.
Y… y parten para luna de miel o se quedan una noche de hotel en algún lado en la ciudad.	51	And… leave for their honeymoon or stay the night at a hotel somewhere in the city.
Y después al otro día salen de luna de miel.	52	And then, the next day, they depart on their honeymoon.
Así que, bueno, básicamente la comida es lo más importante en un casamiento.	53	So, you know, food is basically the most important thing at a wedding.

*11 A *sulky* is a two-wheeled horse-drawn wagon

*13 *picada* = a tray of slices of cured meat and cheese, similar to a charcuterie board.

*46 *carioca* (invariable adjective) = of Rio de Janeiro

Vocabulary

1. wedding[2] _____
2. trendy, in style[3] _____
3. countryside[5] _____
4. homemade[8] _____
5. rural[10] _____
6. roasted[12] _____
7. enclosed[14] _____
8. charms[20] _____
9. ring[21] _____
10. single[23] _____
11. separate[24] _____
12. ring[27] _____
13. bouquet[28] _____
14. custom[31] _____
15. garter[31] _____
16. bride[32] _____
17. groom[33] _____
18. to enjoy oneself[35] _____
19. to revolve around[38] _____
20. a sign[39] _____
21. to happen[40] _____
22. parents[44] _____
23. confetti[47] _____
24. party favors[47] _____
25. to realize[49] _____
26. to sneak away[50] _____
27. honeymoon[52] _____

Translate

1. En Buenos Aires los casamientos en general son *de noche / a noche.*
2. Hace unos años atrás se *empezó / empizo* a poner de moda los casamientos de día.
3. Los casamientos usualmente se hacen en *las afueras / afuera* de la ciudad.
4. Todo el casamiento fue *en torno a / entorno de* lo campestre.
5. *Después / Déspues* se hizo la ceremonia.
6. Los novios se retiran antes *de / que* terminar la fiesta.

notes

True or False: 1. T² 2. F¹¹ 3. T³⁶ 4. T⁴⁰ 5. F⁴⁸ **Expressions:** a veces - sometimes / al mediodía - at noon / antes - before / así que - so, therefore / bueno - well / de noche - at night / después - afterward, then / destacable - remarkable / durante el día - in the daytime / en ese sentido - in that sense / en forma abundante - in abundance / en torno a - around, surrounding / hace unos años atrás - a few years ago / hacia atrás - back(ward) / incluso - even / lo más importante - the most important thing / toda la noche - all night / un poco más - a bit more / usualmente - usually / y así - and so on **Multiple Choice:** 1. c⁸ 2. a²⁷ d³⁰ 3. b⁵³ **Vocabulary:** 1. casamiento 2. de moda 3. campo 4. casero 5. campestre 6. asado 7. cerrado 8. dijes 9. anillo 10. soltero 11. aparte 12. anillo 13. ramo 14. costumbre 15. liga 16. novia 17. novio 18. disfrutar 19. girar en torno a 20. una señal 21. suceder 22. padres 23. papel picado 24. cotillón 25. enterarse 26. irse a escondidas 27. luna de miel **Translate:** 1. de noche² In Buenos Aires, weddings are generally at night. 2. empezó³ A few years ago, daytime weddings started to come into style. 3. las afueras⁴ The weddings are usually done on the outskirts of the city. 4. en torno a¹⁰ The whole wedding was rural-themed. 5. Después¹⁴ Then the ceremony took place. 6. de⁴⁸ The bride and groom leave before the party is over.

Temas Sociales

El Sistema de Salud en Costa Rica

Laura (Costa Rica)
356 words (120 wpm) — 25

True or False

1. In Costa Rica, medical care and healthcare programs are out of the reach of the poorest citizens. T☐ F☐
2. Costa Rica is now considered a first-world country. T☐ F☐
3. There are over 1,000 central hospitals in Costa Rica. T☐ F☐
4. Costa Rica has the third most developed social security system in Latin America. T☐ F☐
5. Because of the poor healthcare system, many Costa Ricans travel to neighboring countries for medical procedures. T☐ F☐

Expressions

aún	basically
básicamente	I believe that
como por ejemplo	it serves to
creo que	it works
debemos de estar orgullosos	more than
en promedio	nevertheless
funciona	on average
más de	percentage
porcentaje	still
sin embargo	such as
sirve para	we must be proud

Multiple Choice

1. In Costa Rica, the healthcare system is funded by ___.
   a. the Costa Rican government
   b. workers' contributions
   c. U.N. funds
   d. *none of the above*

2. Which <u>two</u> of the following does Laura mention?
   a. that children are covered under their parents' policies
   b. the percentage of one's salary that goes toward the healthcare system
   c. the year that the current healthcare system was introduced
   d. that Costa Ricans are proud of their healthcare system

3. In Costa Rica, life expectancy is around ___ years.
   a. 69   b. 76   c. 79   d. 86

Text

Nuestro sistema de salud en Costa Rica es algo de lo que todos los ticos y ticas estamos muy orgullosos.	1	Our healthcare system in Costa Rica is something that all Costa Ricans are very proud of,
porque es un sistema muy inclusivo.	2	because it is a very inclusive system.
Es un sistema que... que de verdad le llega a la gente.	3	It is a system that... that really reaches the people.
Se han hecho muchos logros con poco dinero,	4	There have been a lot of achievements without a lot of money,
porque pues Costa Rica es un país del tercer mundo,	5	because, well, Costa Rica is a third-world country,
no contamos con tantas... con tanto financiamiento, con tanto aporte económico,	6	we don't have much... much financing or economic support;
pero sin embargo es comparable con sistemas de salud de países como Canadá o inclusive Estados Unidos.	7	nevertheless, it is comparable to healthcare systems in countries like Canada or even the United States.
Básicamente los trabajadores aportan un porcentaje de su salario,	8	Basically, workers contribute with a percentage of their salaries,
y entonces brindan seguro a ellos mismos y a sus familiares, a sus hijos menores de dieciocho años,	9	to provide healthcare for themselves, their families, and their children under 18 years old,
o incluso hijos mayores de dieciocho años que sean aún estudiantes pues también están cubiertos.	10	or even adult children over 18 who are still students are also covered.
Además ese aporte también sirve para cubrir personas, por ejemplo, que no tienen hogar, las que andan en las calles, indigentes o los inmigrantes, que también son atendidos, las mujeres embarazadas, los niños y los adultos mayores.	11, 12	In addition, this contribution also serves to cover people, for example, who are homeless, those who are on the streets, the poor, or immigrants, who are also treated, pregnant women, children, and the elderly.
Todas esas poblaciones son atendidos en cualquier hospital, sin cargos, y sin preguntas, verdad.	13	All these people are treated in any hospital, without charge, and without question, really.
Es... este, nuestro... nuestro sistema cuenta con hospitales, verdad obviamente hospitales centrales,	14	Um... our... our system has hospitals, really, obviously central hospitals.
que son más de veinticinco, creo que veintinueve, no recuerdo exactamente,	15	There are over 25, 29 I think—I don't remember the exact number,
pero también cuenta con hospitales especializados,	16	but it also has specialized hospitals
como por ejemplo el hospital de niños o el hospital de la mujer, el hospital del adulto mayor.	17	such as The Children's Hospital, The Women's Hospital, The Elderly Hospital.
En fin hay también hospitales con sus especializaciones, y, bueno, funciona.	18	Anyway, there are also hospitals with their specializations, and, well, it works.
Tenemos como hospitales o clínicas comunitarias,	19	We also have small community hospitals or clinics,

que creo que son más de mil, las que hay en todo el país,	20	which I believe number over 1,000 in the country as a whole,
que funcionan a nivel más pequeño, verdad, de comunidades.	21	that function on a smaller scale, really, for communities.
Las personas ahí se atienden sus necesidades generales, como consultas generales,	22	There, people have their overall needs met, as well as general inquiries,
Verdad, con su médico, sus enfermeras y realmente funciona.	23	with their professional doctor and nurses, and this really works.
O sea, la gente tiene su… su acceso a programas de salud muy buenos,	24	In other words, people have… access to very good health programs,
y es algo por lo que de verdad debemos de estar muy orgullosos.	25	and it is something that we really should be very proud of.
Incluso creo que somos el tercer país con una seguridad social más desarrollada en América Latina.	26	We even have the third most developed social security in Latin America.
Y nuestra esperanza de vida, o sea en promedio, es de setenta y nueve.	27	And our life expectancy is, at least on average, is around 79,
Es la mayor en toda América Latina.	28	the longest in all of Latin America.
Entonces, muy orgullosos de nuestro sistema de salud.	29	So [we are] very proud of our healthcare system.

Vocabulary

1. proud[1] _____
2. healthcare system[1] _____
3. to reach[3] _____
4. to have[6] _____
5. to provide[9] _____
6. poor[12] _____
7. the elderly[12] _____
8. pregnant[12] _____
9. treated[13] _____
10. nurse[23] _____
11. developed[26] _____

Translate

1. En Costa Rica todos *están / son* muy orgullosos de su sistema de salud.
2. Es un sistema que *de / en* verdad le llega a la gente.
3. Se han *hecho / hacido* muchos logros con poco dinero.
4. No contamos *con / -* tanto financiamiento.
5. Hay más *de / que* veinticinco hospitales.
6. Eso es algo por lo que de verdad debemos *de / que* estar muy orgullosos.

True or False: 1. F[2] 2. F[5] 3. F[15,20] 4. T[26] 5. F[29] **Expressions:** aún - still / basicamente - basically / como por ejemplo - such as / creo que - I believe that / debemos de estar orgullosos - we must be proud / en promedio - on average / funciona - it works / más de - more than / porcentaje - percentage / sin embargo - nevertheless / sirve para - it serves to / **Multiple Choice:** 1. b[8] 2. a[9,29] 3. c[27] **Vocabulary:** 1. orgulloso 2. sistema de salud 3. llegar a 4. contar con 5. brindar 6. indigente 7. adultos mayores 8. embarazada 9. atendidos 10. enfermera 11. desarrollado **Translate:** 1. están[1] In Costa Rica, everyone is very proud of their healthcare system. 2. de[3] It is a system that really reaches people. 3. hecho[4] Many achievements have been made with little money. 4. con[6] We do not have much financing. 5. de[15] There are more than twenty-five hospitals. 6. de[25] That is something that we really must be very proud of.

notes

La Pobreza

Jorge (Peru)
273 words (106 wpm)   26

True or False

1. Jorge feels that poverty is the biggest social issue in his country. T☐ F☐
2. According to Jorge, the Peruvian government has now established effective social policies to combat poverty. T☐ F☐
3. Many Peruvians still have faith in politicians to bring about change. T☐ F☐
4. Peru has a strong educational system. T☐ F☐
5. The current Peruvian government is making meaningful investments to improve the educational system. T☐ F☐

Expressions

a lo que yo voy	at the end
adelante	hardly ever
al final	in front of- ahead
casi nunca	it's a little sad
en la actualidad	more than anything
es un poco triste	nowadays
esperanzarse en alguien	they just turn out to be words
llevar pan a la mesa	to be able to buy food for you and your family
lo que yo veo	to put one's hopes in someone
mas que nada	what I see
sin precedentes	where I'm going with this
solo resultan ser palabras	without precedent

Multiple Choice

1. In recent years, Peru has ___.
   a. suffered a serious economic recession and mass unemployment
   b. outpaced other South American countries in economic growth
   c. elected a government whose main agenda is to eradicate poverty
   d. *none of the above*

2. Which of the following does Jorge <u>not</u> mention as an issue facing the poor in Peru?
   a. inequality   c. discrimination against ethnic minorities
   b. poor family planning   d. inadequate education

3. Jorge says that poor mothers often __ to make ends meet.
   a. sell candy on the streets   c. sell their children
   b. resort to prostitution   d. shoplift and pickpocket

103 | Spanish Voices 2

Text

El problema social más grande de mi país, para mí, es la pobreza.	1	The biggest social issue in my country, in my opinion, is poverty.
Eh... en los últimos años, el Perú ha crecido económicamente sin precedentes a comparación del resto de países de Sudamérica.	2	Uh... in recent years, Peru has grown economically without precedent in comparison to the rest of the countries in South America.
A lo que yo voy es, si la cosas mejoran, ¿por qué hay tantas cosas que parecen no mejorar?	3	Where I'm going with this is, if things are getting better, why are there so many things that seem not to be improving?
Eh... yo creo que esto se debe más que nada a la pobre política social que ejerce el gobierno,	4	Uh... I believe that this is due, more than anything, to poor social policy exercised by the government,
como es la política a veces, ¿no?	5	as it is with politics sometimes, right?
Eh... la gente se esperanza en alguien que promete un cambio.	6	Uh... people put their hopes in someone who promises change,
Bueno, pero al final de todo, solo resultan ser palabras, ¿no?	7	Well, but at the end of it all, they just turn out to be words, yeah?
Hay mucha gente que busca el desarrollo, la mejoría, pero eso nunca... casi nunca se da,	8	There are a lot of people looking for development, improvement, but that never... hardly ever occurs,
porque acá no hay mucha inclusión; hay mucha desigualdad.	9	because here there isn't much inclusiveness; there's inequality.
Limitan a la gente con una educación muy pobre,	10	They limit people with very poor education.
lo que yo veo en la actualidad, en nuestra realidad, es que la planificación familiar es muy pobre,	11	What I see nowadays, in our reality, is that family planning is very poor,
porque tú habrías de tener más hijos de los que puedes mantener.	12	because you'd have more children than you can support.
Es muy normal estar en el centro de la ciudad,	13	It's quite normal to be downtown,
y tú ves a una madre con dos niños caminando adelante de ella, uno en la espalda,	14	and you see a mother with two children walking in front of her, one on her back,
vendiendo golosinas, para poder llevar un pan a la mesa,	15	selling candy to put food on the table,
porque el gobierno no destina más fondos a... a campañas sociales, ¿no?	16	because the government doesn't allocate more funds to... to social campaigns, right?
Implementar la educación, formar a la gente desde... desde que son niños, ¿no?	17	To implement education, educate people from... starting when they are children, huh?
para que tengan mayores recursos, ¿no?,	18	So that they have better resources, yeah?
se puedan... se tengan acceso a conocimiento que les permita aspirar a algo mejor en la vida, ¿no?	19	[and] can... have access to knowledge that allows them to aspire to something better in life, right?
Pero es un poco triste de que nuestro país es tan rico en tantos aspectos,	20	But it's a little sad that our country is so rich in so many ways,
pero a la vez somos pobres en otros.	21	but at the same time, we're poor in others.

Vocabulary

1. to turn out[7] _____
2. development[8] _____
3. improvement[8] _____
4. inequality[9] _____
5. to support[12] _____
6. candy[15] _____
7. to allocate funds[16] _____
8. social campaigns[16] _____
9. to educate[17] _____
10. knowledge[19] _____
11. to allow[19] _____

Translate

1. Un problema social es la *pobreza / pobredad*.
2. Yo creo que esto se debe más que *qualquier / qualquiera cosa* a la política social que ejerce el gobierno.
3. La gente se esperanza *en / a* alguien que promete un cambio.
4. El gobierno no destina fondos *a / en* campañas sociales.
5. Quieren formar a la gente desde que *son / sean* niños.
6. Nuestro país es *tan / así* rico en tantos aspectos pero a la vez somos pobres en otros.

notes

True or False: 1. T[1] 2. F[4] 3. T[6] 4. F[10] 5. F[16] **Expressions:** a lo que yo voy - where I'm going with this / adelante - in front of- ahead / al final - at the end / casi nunca - hardly ever / en la actualidad - nowadays / es un poco triste - it's a little sad / esperanzarse en alguien - to put one's hopes in someone / llevar pan a la mesa - to be able to buy food for you and your family / lo que yo veo - what I see / mas que nada - more than anything / sin precedentes - without precedent / solo resultan ser palabras - they just turn out to be words **Multiple Choice:** 1. b[2] 2. c[9-11] 3. a[14-15] **Vocabulary:** 1. resultar 2. desarrollo 3. mejoría 4. desigualdad 5. mantener 6. golosinas 7. destinar fundos 8. campañas sociales 9. formar 10. conocimiento 11. permitir **Translate:** 1. pobreza[1] A social problem is poverty. 2. qualquier[4] I believe that this is due, more than anything, to the social policy exercised by the government. 3. en[6] People put their hopes in someone who promises change. 4. a[16] The government does not allocate funds to social campaigns. 5. son[17] They want to educate people from the time they are children. 6. tan[20] Our country is so rich in so many aspects, but, at the same time, we are poor in others.

La Discriminación

Sandra (Mexico)
440 words (131 wpm) 27

True or False

1. Sandra specifically talks about discrimination against Hispanics in the US. T☐ F☐
2. She implies that immigrants often do difficult work for low pay. T☐ F☐
3. Some people have been arrested because they didn't have proper ID. T☐ F☐
4. The US government is doing better at combatting discrimination. T☐ F☐
5. Sandra tells us about a time she was discriminated against for speaking Spanish in public. T☐ F☐

Expressions

arreglar la situación	for no reason
creo que esto no es verdad	I think that's not true
la gente se queja de	in the future
más adelante	little or nothing
poco o nada	people complain about
quitar	to fix the situation
sin ninguna razón	to take away

Multiple Choice

1. Sandra mentions that people in the U.S. complain that immigrants ___.
   a. commit crimes
   b. take jobs from Americans
   c. do not learn English
   d. do not pay taxes

2. According to Sandra, undocumented immigrants ___.
   a. often pay more taxes than those working legally
   b. usually underreport their earnings in order to pay less tax
   c. do not pay taxes because they do not have access to education and healthcare
   d. *none of the above*

3. Sandra implies that some Hispanics ___ to avoid discrimination.
   a. pay bribes
   b. have returned to their home countries
   c. try to assimilate
   d. *all of the above*

Text

Es muy bien conocido que existe bastante discriminación hacia los hispanos aquí en los Estados Unidos.	1	It's very well known that quite a bit of discrimination exists towards Hispanics here in the United States.
Y yo he escuchado muchas veces que principalmente la gente se queja de que los inmigrantes vienen a quitarles los empleos a la gente de aquí.	2	And I have heard many times that mainly people complain about immigrants coming to take jobs from people here.

Pero creo que esto no es verdad ya que los inmigrantes que vienen y trabajan aquí hacen trabajos que mucha gente no quiere... no quiere realizar.	3	But I don't think that's true since immigrants that come and work here do jobs that many people don't want to... don't want to do.
Y por el pago que reciben yo creo que nadie haría el tipo de trabajos que ellos eh... realizan por el pago que reciben.	4	And for the pay they receive, I don't think anyone would do the kind of work that they uh... do for the pay they get.
Entonces no creo que ese sea el problema que vienen a quitar empleos,	5	So, I don't think that's the problem, that they come to take jobs,
más bien si... si no existieran yo creo que habría... se... habría muchos empleos que nadr-... que nadie querría tomar por el tipo de empleos que son y por la paga que se recibe.	6	but more likely if... if they weren't here, I think there would be... they... there would be many jobs that nobody... that nobody would want to take because of the kind of job they are and what is paid.
Eh... estas personas, aún... que trabajan aquí y pagan impuestos aún siendo indocumentados, no tienen el mismo acceso a la educación o a los servicios de salud que tiene un trabajador normal.	7	Uh... these people, even though... they work here and pay taxes even though they are undocumented, don't have the same access to education or to healthcare services as a normal worker has.
Y muchas veces hasta pagan más impuesto-... impuestos que un trabajador eh... legal.	8	And many times, they even pay more taxes than a legal eh... worker.
Últimamente en algunos estados se han adoptado nuevas leyes y políticas que afectan a los indocumentados.	9	Lately, in some states, they have adopted new laws and policies that affect undocumented people.
Tal es el caso de... de Arizona, ¿no? donde se ve bastante discriminación,	10	Such is the case in... in Arizona, right?—where you can see a lot of discrimination,
donde las personas son detenidas solamente por su aspecto.	11	where people get arrested just because of the way they look.
Las detienen sin ninguna razón, solamente porque su aspecto es de... de... de hispano.	12	They arrest them for no reason, only because they look... Hispanic.
Y se cometen muchas injusticias en contra de ellos.	13	And many injustices are committed against them.
Con mucha tristeza yo... yo he podido saber de casos...	14	With great sadness I... I have known some cases...
he conocido a personas que deciden no enseñar a sus hijos el español o no les inculcan la cultura de su país,	15	I have met people that have decided not to teach Spanish to their children, or they don't instill the culture of their [home] country,
porque creen que de esta forma sus hijos van a ser discriminados,	16	because they think if they do, their children will be discriminated against,
En lugar de... de enseñarles su idioma y su cultura para tener una ventaja más adelante.	17	instead of teaching their language and their culture so as to have an advantage in the future.
Es muy triste darse cuenta que eso consideran que es algo que les va a afectar más adelante en lugar de beneficiarlos por saber un adioma-... idioma adicional.	18	It's very sad to realize that they consider that to be something that will affect them later instead of benefiting them for knowing an additional lu... language.
También es triste ver cómo el gobierno ha hecho poco o nada para ayudar a estas	19	It's also sad to see how the government has done little or nothing to help these people that form a part of the country's economy.

personas que forman parte de la economía del país.		
Y solamente son utilizadas en el momento de elecciones.	20	And they are only used at election time.
Se les prometen muchas cosas para ganar sus votos,	21	They make them a lot of promises to get their votes,
pero al final del día no se hace nada para arreglar esta situación.	22	but at the end of the day, nothing is done to fix the situation.
Como mexicana viviendo aquí en los Estados Unidos si me he dado cuenta de que existen muchos estereotipos hacia la gente hispana que no son nada positivos.	23	As a Mexican living here in the United States, I have realized that there are a lot of stereotypes towards Hispanic people that are not at all positive.
Y es muy triste ver que se generaliza y se discrimina de esa forma a toda la gente de origen hispano.	24	And it's sad to see that it's widespread, and people of Hispanic origin are discriminated against like this.

Vocabulary

1. salary[6] _____
2. job[6] _____
3. taxes[7] _____
4. healthcare services[7] _____
5. policy[9] _____
6. law[9] _____
7. arrested[11] _____
8. to realize[18] _____
9. to benefit[18] _____
10. to make a promise[21] _____
11. stereotype[23] _____

Translate

1. Es muy bien conocido que *existe / exista* bastante discriminación hacia los inmigrantes aquí en los Estados Unidos.
2. La gente se queja *de / en* que los inmigrantes vienen a quitarles los empleos a la gente de aquí.
3. Yo creo que nadie *haría / hiciera* el tipo de trabajos que ellos realizan por el pago que reciben.
4. Entonces no creo que ese *sea / es* el problema.
5. Les enseñan su idioma y su cultura para *- / que* tener una ventaja más adelante.
6. Me he dado cuenta de *- / lo* que existen muchos estereotipos hacia la gente hispana.

notes

True or False: 1. T[1] 2. T[3-4] 3. F[10-12] 4. F[19-22] 5. F **Expressions:** arreglar la situación - to fix the situation / creo que esto no es verdad - I think that's not true / la gente se queja de - people complain about / más adelante - in the future / poco o nada - little or nothing / quitar - to take away / sin ninguna razón - for no reason **Multiple Choice:** 1. b[2] 2. a[8] 3. c[15] **Vocabulary:** 1. paga/pago 2. empleo 3. impuestos 4. servicios de salud 5. política 6. ley 7. detenido 8. darse cuenta 9. beneficiar 10. prometer 11. estereotipo **Translate:** 1. existe[1] It is very well known that there is quite a bit of discrimination toward immigrants here in the United States. 2. de[2] People complain that immigrants come to take jobs away from people here. 3. haría[4] I don't think that anybody would do the kind of jobs they do for the pay they receive. 4. sea[5] So, I don't think that's the problem. 5. -[17] They teach them their language and culture to give them an advantage later. 6. -[23] I have realized that there are many stereotypes toward Hispanics.

La Migración Ilegal de Niños

José (Honduras)
442 words (172 wpm) — 28

True or False

1. Neighboring countries illegally send their children to Honduras.   T ☐ F ☐
2. The majority of child immigrants have been from Honduras.   T ☐ F ☐
3. José mentions some dangers involved in illegal immigration.   T ☐ F ☐
4. Child emigration is a growing problem in Honduras.   T ☐ F ☐
5. Some parents would go to the US first and then send for their children.   T ☐ F ☐

Expressions

como les decía	as I said
en el camino	he managed to arrive
gracias a Dios	it was common
ha habido	on the way
logró llegar	please
por favor	thank God
se daba bastante	there have been
se sienten obligados	they feel obliged

Multiple Choice

1. José mentions that a common reason why children are sent to the US is ___.
    a. to work and send home money
    b. to avoid being forced into street gangs
    c. for a better education
    d. to get to know relatives

2. The president of Honduras asked parents ___.
    a. to send their children to the US to work and send money back to Honduras
    b. to stop sending their children to the US because of the dangers involved
    c. to have fewer children if they cannot support them financially
    d. *none of the above*

3. José says that ___ once had to travel to the US illegally and alone to join his mother there.
    a. he himself
    b. his best friend
    c. his nephew
    d. one of his students

Text

Un problema social que se daba bastante en nuestro país, que gracias a Dios ya casi no se da, era la inmigración de niños.	1	A social problem that was common in our country, [but] thank God hardly occurs [now], was the immigration of children.
En Latinoamérica, sabemos que eso es un problema, la inmigración ilegal hacia Estados Unidos.	2	In Latin America, we know that that's a problem, illegal immigration to the United States.
Hemos escuchado historias sobre personas que pierden la vida,	3	We have heard stories about people who lose their lives,

personas que son mutiladas en el viaje hacia el Norte.	4	people who are mutilated on the trip to the north.
En Honduras teníamos el problema que mandaban los niños.	5	In Honduras, we had a problem with people sending children.
Había padres que se iban ellos primero.	6	There were parents that they were going first.
Pagaban un coyote, se quedaban en Estado Unidos, y luego mandaban a los niños,	7	They'd pay a coyote, stay in the U.S., and then send for their children,
o les pedían a los niños que ellos se fueran también.	8	or they'd ask their children to go [themselves].
Y en el camino, las oficinas de migración o la policía de migración, se encontró varios niños que iban solos.	9	And on the way, the immigration offices, or immigration police, found several children that were traveling alone.
La mayoría de estos eran hondureños, de mi país.	10	Most of these were Hondurans from my country.
Entonces, ¿por qué razón los niños emigran?	11	So, for what reason do children emigrate?
Bueno, como les decía: los papás se van primero o los mismos papás desde aquí, desde Honduras,	12	Well, as I said, the parents go first, or they stay here in Honduras,
ellos mandan a los niños allá al Norte a buscar otros familiares porque esos niños no van a la escuela.	13	[and] they send the children up north to find other relatives because these children do not attend school.
Esos niños no tienen cómo ir a la escuela.	14	These children have no way to go to school.
No tienen ropa, por la condición económica de ellos mismos, de los padres.	15	They don't have clothes, due to the economic condition of themselves, of their parents.
Los papás se sienten obligados a mandarlos o a mandarlos a traer una vez que ellos ya han logrado cruzar la frontera.	16	Parents feel obliged to send for them or have them brought up once they have already managed to cross the border.
Fue tanto así el fenómeno que la Presidencia de la República empezó a hacer una campaña	17	The phenomenon was to the point that the President of the Republic began a campaign
donde pedía a los padres que por favor no enviara a sus niños de forma ilegal,	18	in which he asked parents to, please, not send their children illegally
porque... por todos los peligros a que se exponen.	19	because... because of all the dangers they face.
Pero sí ha sido un problema aquí en mi país, la inmigración ilegal de niños.	20	But it has been a problem here in my country, the illegal immigration of children.
Siempre se da la inmigración ilegal de adultos.	21	Illegal immigration of adults always happens.
Eso se da casi en todos los países de Latinoamérica.	22	This occurs in almost all Latin American countries.
Pero en mi país particularmente se dio mucho la inmigración ilegal de niños.	23	But in my country particularly, the illegal immigration of children was occurring a lot.
Creo que en estos momentos ya no se da tanto, pero sí, siempre tenemos niños...	24	I don't think right now it's going on as much, but we do always have children...
Yo tuve la experiencia, o en la escuela donde yo trabajo tuvimos la experiencia, que hubo niños que se fueron de forma ilegal.	25	I had the experience, or in the school where I work, we had the experience of children that were going illegally.

Bueno, hubo un estudiante de hecho, que era estudiante mío, que su mamá, que ya estaba en Estados Unidos, le mandó a decir:	26	Well, there was a student in fact, who was my student, whose mother, who was already in the United States, sent for him, saying:
"Bueno m'ijo, yo necesito que usted se vaya, que cruce la frontera".	27	Well, son, I need you to leave, to cross the border.
Al día siguiente el muchacho se fue.	28	The next day the boy had gone.
Logró llegar gracias a Dios pero aun así, se expuso a muchos peligros y no todos los niños pueden tener la misma suerte.	29	He made it, thank God, but still, he was exposed to many dangers, and not all children have the same luck.
Ha habido niños que se han encontrado deportados y han tenido que regresar,	30	There have been children who have found themselves deported and had to return,
niños que se han deshidratado, se han desmayado en medio del desierto.	31	children who were dehydrated, have fainted in the desert.
Y ese es un problema que hemos tenido aquí en mi país.	32	And that's a problem we've had here in my country.

Vocabulary

1. to present itself, happen[1] _____
2. clothes[15] _____
3. to manage to[16] _____
4. danger[19] _____
5. to happen[21] _____
6. little boy[28] _____
7. luck[29] _____
8. dehydrated[31] to _____
9. faint[31] _____
10. in the middle of[31] _____

Translate

1. Les pedían a los niños que ellos se *fueran / irían* también.
2. *¿Por qué / Porque* razón los niños emigran?
3. Se pedía a los padres que por favor no *enviara / envíe* a sus niños de forma ilegal.
4. Siempre se *da / va* la inmigración ilegal de adultos.
5. Gracias a Dios logró *llegar / llegando*.
6. Ha *habido / hubido* niños que se han encontrado deportados y han tenido que regresar.

notes

True or False: 1. F[2] 2. T[10] 3. T[30-31] 4. F[24] 5. T[6-7] **Expressions:** como les decía - as I said / en el camino - on the way / gracias a Dios - thank God / ha habido - there have been / logró llegar - he managed to arrive / por favor - please / se daba bastante - it was common / se sienten obligados - they feel obliged **Multiple Choice:** 1. c[13-15] 2. b[17-18] 3. d[26] **Vocabulary:** 1. darse 2. ropa 3. lograr 4. peligro 5. darse 6. muchacho 7. suerte 8. deshidratado 9. desmayarse 10. en medio del **Translate:** 1. fueran[8] They asked the children to go, too. 2. por qué[11] Why do children emigrate? 3. enviara[18] Parents were asked to please not send their children illegally. 4. da[21] Illegal immigration of adults always happens. 5. llegar[29] Thank God he made it. 6. habido[30] There have been children who have found themselves deported and had to go back.

La Violencia Doméstica

Francisco (Spain)
305 words (147 wpm) 29

True or False

1. Gender-based violence is a much bigger problem in underdeveloped countries than in developed countries. T ☐ F ☐
2. According to Francisco, social problems tend to decrease as a country develops. T ☐ F ☐
3. He implies that domestic violence is most often committed by men against women. T ☐ F ☐
4. People tend to start to manifest signs of being abusive in childhood or adolescence. T ☐ F ☐
5. Francisco admits to being a victim of domestic violence himself. T ☐ F ☐

Expressions

asuntos privados	(starting) from
dentro de	common
desde	either
frecuente	gender-based violence
nada más lejos de la realidad	it's always been this way
no son conscientes	nothing is further from reality
siempre ha sido así	once
tampoco	private affairs
una vez	they're not aware
violencia de género	within

Multiple Choice

1. Francisco mentions that victims may not realize they are being abused ___.

    a. because they think it's normal and culturally acceptable behavior in society.
    b. when it is verbal and emotional abuse, and not physical abuse
    c. if they themselves are also abusers
    d. *none of the above*

2. Francisco mentions that victims may not report the abuse because ___.

    a. their neighbors will gossip
    b. they are afraid or ashamed
    c. the police will do nothing to help
    d. *all of the above*

3. Which of the following statements would Francisco agree with?

    a. People should not meddle in their neighbors' personal affairs even if they suspect domestic abuse.
    b. Many women falsely accuse their husbands of domestic violence when they are bored or unhappy with their marriage.
    c. We should not tolerate domestic violence and should teach our children to do the same.
    d. We should respect that what is considered domestic violence in one culture may be completely normal in another culture.

Text

La violencia de género es uno de los grandes problemas sociales a nivel mundial.	Gender-based violence is one of the greatest social problems in the world.
Afecta a muchísima gente.	It affects a great many people.
Una vez superados en los países desarrollados los grandes peligros de conflicto, como guerras o incluso terrorismo,	Once the great dangers of conflict, such as war or terrorism, [have been] overcome in developed countries,
y rebajados los problemas de violencia en las calles,	and the problems of street violence [has been] reduced,
porque cuando las sociedades adquieren prosperidad, pues, bajan los problemas sociales.	because when societies achieve prosperity, then social problems decrease.
Generalmente, en la sociedad actual nos enfrentamos a un tema del que no se habla mucho,	Generally, in today's society, we face a topic that is not talked about much,
pero que es más frecuente de lo que se suele pensar,	but that is more common than is often thought,
y ocurre en todos los ámbitos sociales.	and it occurs in all social spheres.
La violencia dentro de los hogares, que es nuestra zona más íntima, es una lacra en el mundo entero moderno,	Domestic violence, which is our most intimate area, is a scourge in the entire modern world,
porque hay muchas personas, generalmente mujeres, que son maltratadas dentro de su propia familia	because there are many people, usually women, that are abused within their own families,
(pues por sus maridos, generalmente), que lo sufren,	(usually by their husbands), who suffer.
Pero, o bien no son realmente conscientes de que están siendo maltratadas,	But, either they are not really aware that they are being abused,
pues por temas culturales, porque siempre ha sido así,	due to cultural issues, because it's always been this way,
y se entiende que eso va a ser así;	and it is understood that it will continue being this way;
que hay un género dominante, que es el masculino, y otro género que debe aguantar, que es el femenino,	that there is a dominant sex, the male, and another sex that has to put up with it, the female,
o bien por miedo, o por vergüenza, no se atreven a denunciar a las autoridades estos casos de violencia.	or [it's] out of fear or shame, they do not dare to report these cases to the authorities of violence.
Se dan incluso casos en los que el vecindario sabe de estos maltratos,	There are even cases where neighbors know about the abuse,
pero tampoco lo denuncian, supongo que por esta máxima de:	but they don't report them either, I suppose because of the maxim of
"no meterse en los asuntos privados del vecino, que no nos afectan a nosotros".	not meddling in our neighbor's private affairs, which do not affect us.
Y nada más lejos de la realidad:	But nothing is further from reality:
La violencia dentro de los hogares nos afecta a todos.	Violence within households affects us all.

Es una obligación de todos como ciudadanos enseñar a nuestros hijos a ser intolerantes con este tipo de comportamiento,	22	It is an obligation of all citizens to teach our children to be intolerant of such behavior,
desde la infancia y sobre todo en la adolescencia, que es donde este tipo de abusos empiezan a manifestarse.	23	starting in childhood and particularly during adolescence, which is when this type of abuse begins to manifest itself.
A ver si así, entre todos, evitamos estos comportamientos y conseguimos una sociedad mejor.	24	Let's see if, together, we can avoid this kind of behavior and make a better society.

Vocabulary

1. danger[3]   _____
2. to reduce[4]   _____
3. to achieve[5]   _____
4. to face[6]   _____
5. home[9]   _____
6. scourge[9]   _____
7. abused[10]   _____
8. aware[12]   _____
9. to put up with[15]   _____
10. fear[16]   _____
11. shame[16]   _____
12. to dare[16]   _____
13. neighbors[17]   _____
14. to meddle in[19]   _____

Translate

1. La violencia de género es *uno de los / una de las* grandes problemas a nivel mundial.
2. Afecta *a / -* muchísima gente.
3. Hay muchas personas, generalmente mujeres, que son maltratadas dentro *de / a* su propia familia.
4. Las mujeres no se *atreven / atrevan* a denunciar a las autoridades estos casos de violencia.
5. Se dan incluso casos en los que el vecindario sabe *de / -* estos maltratos.
6. *A / De* ver si conseguimos una sociedad mejor.

notes

True or False: 1. F[1,9] 2. T[10-11] 3. T[5] 4. T[23] 5. F **Expressions:** asuntos privados - private affairs / dentro de - within / desde - (starting) from / frecuente - common / nada más lejos de la realidad - nothing is further from reality / no son conscientes - they're not aware / siempre ha sido así - it's always been this way / tampoco - either / una vez - once / violencia de género - gender-based violence **Multiple Choice:** 1. a[12-14] 2. b[16] 3. c[22-24] **Vocabulary:** 1. peligro 2. rebajar 3. adquirir 4. enfrentar 5. hogar 6. lacra 7. maltratado 8. consciente 9. aguantar 10. miedo 11. vergüenza 12. atreverse 13. vecindario 14. meterse en **Translate:** 1. uno de los[1] Gender-based violence is one of top worldwide problems. 2. a[2] It affects a great many people. 3. de[10] There are many people, usually women, who are abused within their own families. 4. atreven[16] Women do not dare to denounce the authorities in these cases of violence. 5. de[17] There are even cases in which the neighborhood knows of these abuses. 6. a[24] Let's see if we [can] make a better society.

La Economía de Argentina

Florencia (Argentina)
770 words (171 wpm)
30

True or False

1. A lot of rice is produced in the south of Argentina. T☐ F☐
2. Argentina's economy relies more heavily on agriculture than industry. T☐ F☐
3. Florencia is worried about the lack of diversity in Argentina's exports. T☐ F☐
4. It is difficult to buy dollars in Argentina. T☐ F☐
5. Argentina's middle class has been growing in recent years. T☐ F☐

Expressions

a futuro	as things stand
a mi gusto	in my opinion (2x)
en mi punto de vista	in the future
es la única manera	is coming soon
falta poco para	it's the only way
hablar acerca de	not anymore, no longer
hasta el momento	people have to
hoy por hoy	so far
la gente tiene que	to talk about
ya no	

Multiple Choice

1. Florencia mentions that Argentina has been exporting a lot of ___ in recent years.

    a. rice   b. soybeans   c. fruit   d. beef

2. Because Argentina needs to develop its domestic industry, the government ___.

    a. has become protectionist against imports
    b. has allowed foreign companies to operate tax-free inside the country
    c. has signed a free-trade agreement with China
    d. *all of the above*

3. Florencia blames ___ for Argentina's poor economic condition.

    a. geographic isolation   c. a high illiteracy rate
    b. greedy billionaires   d. corruption in politics

Text

Mi nombre es Florencia y soy de Buenos Aires, Argentina.	1	My name is Florencia, and I'm from Buenos Aires, Argentina.
Voy a hablar un poco acerca de la economía del país.	2	I'm going to talk a little about the country's economy.
Argentina es un país, eh... con un territorio muy grande	3	Argentina is a country, uh... with a large territory
que tiene distintos tipos de... de clima lo que permite que tenga distintos tipos de cultivo.	4	that has different types of... of weather that allow it to have various kinds of crops.

Eh... básicamente, es un país cerealero, un país eh... tiene muchas vacas en la parte central;	5	Uh... basically is a grain-producing country, a country... uh... it has a lot of cows in the central region;
en la parte sur, la crianza de ovejas, de frutas, como manzanas, peras, cítricos.	6	in the south, raising sheep, fruit, such as apples, pears, citrus fruit.
Em... en la parte norte, lo que es el arroz, el azúcar, el trigo,	7	Um... in the north, it's rice, sugar, wheat,
pero últimamente, en los últimos años, a partir de... del gran, eh... de la gran demanda de soja, somos eh... "Soja-exportadores".	8	but lately, in recent years, based on... the great... uh... the great demand for soybeans, we are uh... "soy-exporters."
Y es un país que tiene poca industria.	9	And it is a country with little industry.
Yo diría que tiene em... que la gente tiene bastante acceso a la tecnología,	10	I would say it has um... that people have sufficient access to technology,
pero la industria no es eh... lo que más eh... tiene fuerte Argentina.	11	but industry is not uh... uh... what Argentina is strong at.
Hace unos años el país, em... el gobierno empezó a ser más proteccionista de las importaciones,	12	A few years ago, the country, um... the government became more protectionist regarding imports,
por lo cual es muy difícil que insumos y eh... cosas industriales se importen.	13	making it very difficult to import supplies and uh... industrial things.
La idea de eso es poder fomentar la industria nacional	14	The idea is to promote domestic industry,
pero hasta el momento no... no ha surgido o en mi punto de vista, no... no... no se ha desarrollado.	15	but so far, it hasn't come about. In my view, it has not... not... not developed.
Y... con esto de vender la soja y tener una relación eh... una relación comercial con China y con los países del Mercosur eh... ha hecho o ha limitado o ha orientado a la economía hacia... hacia un solo sentido.	16*	And... with this selling soybeans and having a relationship, um... a business relationship with China and Mercosur countries um... has made it or has limited or oriented the economy in... in a single direction.
Em... lo preocupante de eso es el... la poca diversidad de distintas cosas que se exportaban, que se exportan y cosas que antes se exportaban y que ahora ya no se exportan más.	17	Um... what it is worrisome about this is the... the little diversity of different things that were exported... are exported, and things that used to be exported and are now no longer exported.
El tema del dólar es un tema también complicado.	18	The issue of the dollar is a complicated issue too.
Eh... yo me atrevería a decir que la economía es muy parecida a la de Venezuela hoy por hoy,	19	Uh... I would say that the economy is very similar to Venezuela nowadays,
donde a la gente en Argentina le cuesta acceder al dólar,	20	in that for people in Argentina, it is hard to get access to the dollar,
por lo que tiene que... hay mercado paralelo, un mercado en negro eh... donde uno tiene que acudir ahí,	21	which is why there has to... there is a parallel market, or a black market, um... where you have to go there...
para acudir ahí para comprar dólares a un precio más caro que el precio oficial.	22	to go there in order to buy dollars at a higher price than the official rate.

O sea, que si uno va a un banco y dice: "Quiero, todos estos pesos, que me des dólares",	23	That is, if you go to a bank and you say, "I want, with all these pesos, you to give me dollars,"
lo que va a pasar es que uno tiene que demostrar ingresos.	24	what will happen is that you have to prove income.
Uno tiene que decir que uno gana suficientemente dinero como para comprar... como para que esa cantidad de dinero no supere el treinta por ciento de los ingresos.	25	You have to say that you earn enough money to buy... so that that amount of money does not exceed 30% of your income.
Así que es bastante complicado poder acceder a ello.	26	So it is quite difficult to access it.
Aún que yo compre dólares en un banco, no me los van a dar inmediatamente.	27	Even if I still buy dollars in a bank, they're not going to give them to me right away.
Si me los dan inmediatamente, me retienen un treinta y cinco por ciento.	28	If they give me them immediately, they will deduct some 35%.
O sea que el dólar oficial es realmente una... un valor nominal.	29	I mean, the official dollar is really a... a nominal value.
No... no es el precio oficial que tiene el dólar.	30	It is not... not the official value that the dollar has.
Y eh... si yo decido conservar esos dólares en el banco, a plazo fijo y decir... y digo, no los voy a tocar hasta dentro un año, es la única manera en que el dólar tiene el precio oficial, ¿no?	31	And uh... if I choose to keep those dollars in the bank, fixed-term and say... and I say I'm not going to withdraw them within one year, it's the only way to get the dollar at the official rate, yeah?
Es la única manera en que yo a futuro pueda sacar esos dólares al precio oficial.	32	It's the only way I, in the future, can withdraw those dollars at the official rate.
Así que em... la economía no es buena, en el... en el...	33	So um... the economy is not good, in the, in the...
La gente en general tiene em... bajos recursos.	34	People, in general, are um... low-income.
La clase media se ha ido extinguiendo en los últimos años,	35*	The middle class has steadily been dying out in recent years,
la clase alta cada vez más rica; los pobres son más pobres.	36	the upper class richer and richer; the poor poorer and poorer.
Así que falta poco para que haya elecciones.	37	So, we have elections coming up soon.
Vamos a ver si algo cambia en la economía argentina.	38	We'll see if anything changes in Argentina's economy.
Creo que es un país que tiene mucho potencial,	39	I think it's a country that has so much potential
que podría llegar a ser una potencia en el mundo.	40	that it could become a world power.
Pero que la corrupción que hay en la política hace que no seamos bien vistos en el mundo.	41	But corruption in politics makes us unwelcome in the world.
Y el pueblo no ve bien a sus líderes gubernamentales.	42	And people do not view their government leaders in a good way.
Así que eso lo que... es lo que está, a mi gusto, lo que yo pienso,	43	So, that's what... what is, in my opinion, what I think,

eh... no contribuyendo con... con un desarrollo económico eh... de progreso.	44	uh... not contributing with economic development um... of progress.	
Mi nombre es Florencia y soy de Buenos Aires, Argentina.	45	My name is Florencia, and I'm from Buenos Aires, Argentina.	
Voy a hablar un poco acerca de la economía del país.	46	I'm going to talk a little about the country's economy.	
Argentina es un país, eh... con un territorio muy grande	47	Argentina is a country, uh... with a large territory	
que tiene distintos tipos de... de clima lo que permite que tenga distintos tipos de cultivo.	48	that has different types of... of weather that allow it to have various kinds of crops.	
Eh... básicamente, es un país cerealero, un país eh...tiene muchas vacas en la parte central;	49	Uh... basically is a grain-producing country, a country... uh... it has a lot of cows in the central region;	
en la parte sur, la crianza de ovejas, de frutas, como manzanas, peras, cítricos.	50	in the south, raising sheep, fruit, such as apples, pears, citrus fruit.	
Em... en la parte norte, lo que es el arroz, el azúcar, el trigo,	51	Um... in the north, it's rice, sugar, wheat,	
pero últimamente, en los últimos años, a partir de...del gran, eh...de la gran demanda de soja, somos eh... "Soja-exportadores".	52	but lately, in recent years, based on... the great... uh... the great demand for soybeans, we are uh... "soy-exporters."	

*16 *Mercosur* (Mercado Común del Sur) is a South American trade bloc.

*35 *ir* + gerund suggests that an action is proceeding steadily, hence the translation 'steadily' in the English. Here, it's used in the present perfect: *ha ido __-ndo* has been __ing steadily.

Vocabulary

1. crops[4] _____
2. cow[5] _____
3. sheep[5] _____
4. breeding[6] _____
5. apple[6] _____
6. pear[6] _____
7. citrus fruit[6] _____
8. rice[7] _____
10. wheat[7] _____
11. soy[8] _____
12. supplies[13] _____
13. to promote[14] _____
14. business relationship[16] _____
15. worrisome[17] _____
16. to deduct[28] _____
17. the upper class[36] _____

Translate

1. Voy a hablar un poco *acerca / cerca* de la economía del país.
2. Es la única manera en que yo *a / en* futuro pueda sacar esos dólares al precio oficial.
3. Falta poco *para que / porque* haya elecciones.
4. Creo que es un país que *tiene / tenga* mucho potencial.
5. Creo que *podría / podería* llegar a ser una potencia en el mundo.
6. *A / En* mi gusto Argentina podría llegar a ser una potencia en el mundo.

notes

True or False: 1. F[7] 2. T[11] 3. T[17] 4. T[20] 5. F[35] **Expressions:** a futuro - in the future / a mi gusto - in my opinion / en mi punto de vista - in my opinion / es la única manera - it's the only way / falta poco para - is coming soon / hablar acerca de - to talk about / hasta el momento so far / hoy por hoy - as things stand / la gente tiene que - people have to / ya no - not anymore, no longer **Multiple Choice:** 1. b[8] 2. a[12] 3. d[41] **Vocabulary:** 1. cultivo 2. vaca 3. ovejas 4. crianza 5. manzana 6. pera 7. citricos 8. arroz 9. azucar 10. trigo 11. soja 12. insumos 13. fomentar 14. relación comercial 15. preocupante 16. retener 17. la clase alta **Translate:** 1. acerca[2] I'm going to talk a little about the country's economy. 2. a[32] It is the only way in which I, in the future, can withdraw those dollars at the official rate. 3. para que[37] There are elections coming up soon. 4. tiene[39] I think it's a country that has a lot of potential. 5. podría[40] I think it could become a world power. 6. A[43] In my opinion, Argentina could become a world power.

notes

Visit our website for information on current and upcoming titles, free excerpts, and language learning resources.

www.lingualism.com

www.ingramcontent.com/pod-product-compliance
Lightning Source LLC
LaVergne TN
LVHW060135080526
838202LV00050B/4121